MAN:
THE DWELLING
PLACE OF GOD

What it Means to Have
Christ Living in You

MAN:
THE DWELLING
PLACE OF GOD

A. W. Tozer

Compiled by
ANITA M. BAILEY

MOODY PUBLISHERS
CHICAGO

Previously published by Christian Publications, Inc. First
Christian Publications Edition 1966
First WingSpread Publishers Edition 2008
First Moody Publishers Edition 2018

Cover design by Erik M. Peterson
Cover photo by Jabari Timothy on Unsplash

ISBN: 978-1-60066-028-3
LOC Control Number: 2008927046

We hope you enjoy this book from Moody Publishers. Our
goal is to provide high-quality, thought-provoking books
and products that connect truth to your real needs and
challenges. For more information on other books and
products written and produced from a biblical perspective,
go to www.moodypublishers.com or write to:

Moody Publishers
820 N. LaSalle Boulevard
Chicago, IL 60610

7 9 10 8 6

Printed in the United States of America

CONTENTS

ACKNOWLEDGMENTS

Most of the chapters in this book appeared originally as editorials or articles in *The Alliance Witness*, which Dr. Tozer edited for thirteen years. "How to Make Spiritual Progress" was written for the Gideons of Canada and appeared in their publication. "The Communion of Saints" is from the book *Foundation of the Faith*, published by Fleming H. Revell; and "The Saint Must Walk Alone" appeared first in *Eternity* Magazine. We are grateful for the permissions granted to include them in this book.

INTRODUCTION

The supreme interest in the life of A.W. Tozer was God: He who spoke and brought the world into being, who justly rules over men and nations, yet deigns to make man His dwelling place. He believed that all that really matters is for man to be in right relationship with God, that his first duty—and privilege—is to "glorify God and enjoy Him forever." For this reason he delighted to speak to men of God's majesty and wonder and grace, and he ever sought to instruct and exhort Christians to let this be the purpose of their lives. He grieved that they should be content with less.

Nothing he preached or wrote was merely academic or theoretical. What he said about God came out of many hours spent in His presence and with His Word. What he wrote about men was what he knew of his own heart and observed in others. With the Spirit's anointing came discernment; perception and clarity issued out of a disciplined mind. A broad knowledge averted dullness, and a lively wit brought freshness.

The chapters in this book deal with many aspects of one subject: the relationship of God and man. They are above all practical, and all who read them will profit.

Anita M. Bailey
Managing Editor
Alliance Witness

Man: The Dwelling Place of God

Deep inside every man there is a private sanctum where dwells the mysterious essence of his being. This far-in reality is that in the man which is what it is of itself, without reference to any other part of the man's complex nature. It is the man's "I Am," a gift from the I AM who created him.

The I AM which is God is underived and self-existent; the "I Am" which is man is derived from God and dependent every moment upon His creative fiat for its continued existence. One is the Creator, high over all, ancient of days, dwelling in light unapproachable. The other is a creature and, though privileged beyond all others, is still but a creature, a pensioner on God's bounty and a suppliant before His throne.

The deep-in human entity of which we speak is called in the Scriptures *the spirit of man*. "For what man knoweth the things of a man, save the spirit of man which is in him? even so the things of God knoweth no man, but the Spirit of God" (1 Corinthians 2:11). As God's self-knowledge lies in the eternal Spirit, so man's self-knowledge is by his own spirit, and his knowledge of God is by the direct impression of the Spirit of God upon the spirit of man.

The importance of all this cannot be overestimated as we think and study and pray. It reveals the essential spirituality of mankind. It denies that man is a creature having a spirit and declares that he is a spirit having a body. That which makes him a human being is not his body but his spirit, in which the image of God originally lay.

One of the most liberating declarations in the New Testament is this:

> The true worshippers shall worship the Father in spirit and in truth: for the Father seeketh such to worship him. God is a Spirit: and they that worship him must worship him in spirit and in truth. (John 4:23-24)

Here the nature of worship is shown to be wholly spiritual. True religion is removed from diet and days, from garments and ceremonies, and placed where it belongs—in the union of the spirit of men with the Spirit of God.

From man's standpoint the most tragic loss suffered in the Fall was the vacating of this inner sanctum by the Spirit of God. At the far-in hidden center of man's being is a bush fitted to be the dwelling place of the Triune God. There God planned to rest and glow with moral and spiritual privilege and must now dwell there alone. For so intimately private is the place that no creature can intrude; no one can enter but Christ, and He will enter only by the invitation of faith. "Behold I stand at the door, and knock: if any man hear my voice, and open the door, I will come in to him, and will sup with him, and he with me" (Revelation 3:20).

By the mysterious operation of the Spirit in the new birth, that which is called by Peter "the divine nature" enters the deep-in core of the believer's heart and establishes residence there. "If any man have not the Spirit of Christ, he is none of his," for "the Spirit itself beareth witness with our spirit, that we are the children of God" (Romans 8:9, 16). Such a one is a true Christian, and only such. Baptism, confirmation, the receiving of the sacraments, church membership—these mean nothing unless the supreme act of God in regeneration also takes place. Religious externals may have a meaning for the God-inhabited soul; for any others they are not only useless but may actually become snares, deceiving them into a false and perilous sense of security.

"Keep thy heart with all diligence" (Proverbs 4:23) is more than a wise saying; it is a solemn charge laid upon us by the One who cares most about us. To it we should give the most careful heed lest at any time we should let it slip.

CHAPTER

2

The Call of Christ

To be called to follow Christ is a high honor; higher indeed than any honor men can bestow upon each other.

Were all the nations of the earth to unite in one great federation and call a man to head that federation, that man would be honored above any other man that ever lived. Yet the humblest man who heeds the call to follow Christ has an honor far above such a man; for the nations of the earth can bestow only such honor as they possess, while the honor of Christ is supreme over all. God has given Him a name that is above every name.

This being true and being known to the heavenly intelligences, the methods we use to persuade men to follow Christ must seem to them extremely illogical if not downright wrong.

Evangelical Christians commonly offer Christ to mankind as a nostrum to cure their ills, a way out of their troubles, a quick and easy means to the achievement of personal ends. They use the right words, but their emphasis is awry. The message is so presented as to leave the hearer with the impression that he is being asked to give up much to gain more. And that is not good, however well intentioned it may be.

What we do is precisely what a good salesman does when he presents the excellence of his product as compared with that of his closest competitor. The customer chooses the better of the two, as who would not? But the weakness of the whole salesmanship technique is apparent: the idea of selfish gain is present in the whole transaction.

Jesus Christ is a Man come to save men. In Him the divine nature is married to our human nature, and wherever human nature exists there is the raw material out of which He makes followers and saints. Our Lord recognizes no classes, high or low, rich or poor, old or young, man or woman; all are human and all are alike in Him. His invitation is to all mankind.

In New Testament times persons from many and varied social levels heard Him call and responded: Peter the fisherman; Levi the publican; Luke the physician; Paul the scholar; Mary the demon possessed; Lydia the businesswoman: Paulus the statesman. A few great and many common persons came. They all came and our Lord received them all in the same way and on the same terms.

From any and every profession or occupation men and women may come if they will. The simple rule is that if the occupation is good, continue in it if you so desire; if it is bad, abandon it at once and seek another. If the call includes detachment from all common pursuits to give full time to the work of the gospel, then no profession or occupation, no matter how good or how noble, must keep us from obeying the call.

The activities in which men engage may be divided into two categories: the morally bad and the morally neutral. The activities of the burglar, the gambler, the dictator, the procurer, the dope addict, the gangster and all who prey upon society are bad; nothing can make them better. The call of Christ is away from all such. This is not to be questioned or debated, but accepted without delay and acted upon at once.

But the majority of our human activities are not evil in themselves; they are neutral. The laborer, the statesman, the housewife, the doctor, the teacher, the engineer—such as these engage in activities that are neither good nor bad. Their moral qualities are imparted by the one who engages in them. So the call of Christ is not away from such things, for they may be sanctified by prayer and faith of the individual, and thus turned into a positive good.

One thing is certain: the call of Christ is always a promotion. Were Christ to call a king from his throne to preach the gospel to some tribe of aborigines, that king would be elevated above anything he had known before. Any movement toward Christ is ascent, and any direction away from Him is down.

Yet though we recognize the honor bestowed upon us, there is no place for pride, for the follower of Christ must shoulder his cross and a cross is an object of shame and a symbol of rejection.

Before God and the angels it is a great honor to follow Christ, but before men it is not so. The Christ the world pretends now to honor was once rejected and crucified by that same world. The great saint is honored only after he is dead. Rarely is he known as a saint while he lives. The plaudits of the world come too late, when he can no longer hear them; and perhaps it is better that way. Not many are selfless enough to endure honor without injury to their souls.

In those early Galilean days Christ's followers heard His call, forsook the old life, attached themselves to His band of disciples. This total commitment was their confirmation of faith. Nothing less would do.

And it is not different today. He calls us to leave the old life and to begin the new. There must never be any vacuum, never any place of neutrality where the world cannot identify us. Peter warming himself at the world's fire and trying to seem unconcerned is an example of the kind of halfway discipleship too many are satisfied with. The martyr leaping up in the arena, demanding to be thrown to the lions along with his suffering brethren, is an example of the only kind of dedication that God approves.

What We Think of Ourselves Is Important

The man who is seriously convinced that he deserves to go to hell is not likely to go there, while the man who believes that he is worthy of heaven will certainly never enter that blessed place.

I use the word "seriously" to accent true conviction and to distinguish it from mere nominal belief.

It is possible to go through life believing that we believe, while actually having no conviction more vital than a conventional creed inherited from our ancestors or picked up from the general religious notions current in our social circle. If this creed requires that we admit our own depravity we do so and feel proud of our fidelity to the Christian faith. But from the way we love, praise and pamper ourselves it is plain enough that we do not consider ourselves worthy of damnation.

A revealing proof of this is seen in the squeamish way religious writers use words. An amusing example is found in a cautious editorial change made in the song "The Comforter Has Come." One stanza reads:

O boundless love divine!
How shall this tongue of mine
To wondering mortals tell
The matchless grace divine—
That I, a child of hell,
Should in His image shine!

That is how Dr. Bottome felt it and that is how he wrote it; and the man who has seen the holiness of God and the pollution of his own heart will sing it as it was written, for his whole inner life will respond to the experience. Even if he cannot find chapter and verse to brand him a child of hell, his heart indicts him and he eagerly accuses himself before God as fit only for perdition. This is to experience something profounder than theology, more painfully intimate than creed, and while bitter and harsh it is true to the man's Spirit illuminated view of himself. In so confessing, the enlightened heart is being faithful to the terrible fact while it is singing its own condemnation. This I believe is greatly pleasing to God.

It is, I repeat, amusing if somewhat distressing to come upon an editorial change in this song, which was made obviously in the interest of correct theology, but is once removed from true moral feeling. In one hymnal it is made to read,

> That I, a child of *SIN*,
>   Should in His image shine!

The fastidious song cobbler who made that alteration simply could not think of himself as ever having been a "child of hell." A finicky choice of words sometimes tells us more about a man than the man knows about himself.

This one instance, if isolated in Christian literature, might not be too significant, but when this kind of thing occurs everywhere as thick as dandelions in a meadow it becomes highly significant indeed. The mincing religious prudery heard in the average pulpit is all a part of this same thing—an unwillingness to admit the depths of our inner depravity. We do not actually assent to God's judgment of us except as we hold it as a superficial creed. When the pressure is on we back out. A child of sin? Maybe. A child of hell? No.

Our Lord told of two men who appeared before God in prayer, a Pharisee who recited his virtues and a publican who beat on his breast and pleaded for mercy. The first was rejected, the other justified.

We manage to live with that story in some degree of comfort only by keeping it at full arm's length and never permitting it to catch hold of our conscience. These two men are long ago dead and their story has become a little religious classic. We are different, and how can anything so remote apply to us? So we reason, on a level only slightly above our unconscious, and draw what comfort we can from the vagueness and remoteness of it all.

But why should we not face up to it? The truth is that this happened not a long while ago, but yesterday, this morning, not far away, but here where some of us last knelt to pray. These two men are not dead, but alive, and are found in the local church, at the missionary convention and the deeper life conference here, now, today.

Every man lives at last by his secret philosophy as an airplane flies on its electric beam. It is the profound conviction that we are wholly unworthy of future blessedness, that we are indeed by nature fitted only for destruction, that leads to true repentance. The man who inwardly believes that he is too good to perish will certainly perish unless he experiences a radical change of heart about himself.

The poor quality of Christian that grows out of our modern evangelistic meeting may be accounted for by the absence of real repentance accompanying the initial spiritual experience of the converts. And the absence of repentance is the result of an inadequate view of sin and sinfulness held by those who present themselves in the inquiry room.

"No fears, no grace," said Bunyan. "Though there is not always grace where there is fear of hell, yet, to be sure, there is no grace where there is no fear of God." And again, "I care not at all for that profession which begins not in heaviness of mind. . . . For the fear of God is the beginning of wisdom, and they that lack the beginning have neither middle nor end."

4

The Once-born and the Twice-born

Classification is one of the most difficult of all tasks.

Even in the realm of religion there are enough lights and shades to make it injudicious to draw too fine a line between men and men. If the religious world were composed of squares of solid black and solid white classification would be easy; but unfortunately it is not.

It is a grave error for us evangelicals to assume that the children of God are all in our communion and that all who are not associated with us are *ipso facto* enemies of the Lord. The Pharisees made that mistake and crucified Christ as a consequence.

With all this in mind, and leaning over backward to be fair and charitable, there is yet one distinction which we dare make, which indeed we *must* make if we are to think the thoughts of God after Him and bring our beliefs into harmony with the Holy Scriptures. That distinction is the one which exists between two classes of human beings, the once-born and the twice-born.

That such a distinction does in fact exist was taught by our Lord with great plainness of speech, in contexts which preclude the possibility that He was merely speaking figuratively. "Except a man be born again, he cannot see the kingdom of God," He said (John 3:3), and the whole chapter where these words are found confirms that He was speaking precisely, setting forth meanings as blunt and downright as it is possible for language to convey.

"Ye must be born again," said Christ. "That which is born of the flesh is flesh; and that which is born of the Spirit is spirit" (3:7, 6). This clear line of demarcation runs through the entire New Testament, quite literally dividing one human being from another and making a distinction as sharp as that which exists between different genera of the animal kingdom.

Just who belongs to one class and who to the other it is not always possible to judge, though the two kinds of life ordinarily separate from each other. Those who are twice-born crystallize around the Person of Christ and cluster together only by the ties of nature, aided by the ties of race or by common political and social interests.

Our Lord warned His disciples that they would be persecuted. "In the world ye shall have tribulation," He said (16:33), and "Blessed are they which are persecuted for righteousness' sake: for theirs is the kingdom of heaven. Blessed are ye, when men shall revile you, and persecute you, and shall say all manner of evil against you falsely, for my sake" (Matthew 5:10-11).

These are only two of many passages of the New Testament warning of persecution or recording the fact of harassment and attack suffered by the followers of the Lord. This same idea runs through the entire Bible from the once-born Cain who slew the twice-born Abel to the book of Revelation where the end of human history comes in a burst of blood and fire.

That hostility exists between the once-born and the twice-born is known to every student of the Bible; the reason for it was stated by Christ when He said, "If ye were of the world, the world would love his own: but because ye are not of the world, but I have chosen you out of the world, therefore the world hateth you" (John 15:19). The rule was laid down by the apostle Paul when he wrote, "But as then he that was born after the flesh persecuted him that was born after the Spirit, even so it is now" (Galatians 4:29).

Difference of moral standards between the once-born and the twice-born, and their opposite ways of life, may be contributing causes of this hostility; but the real cause lies deeper. There are two spirits abroad in the earth: the spirit that works in the children of disobedience and the Spirit of God. These two can never be reconciled in time or in eternity. The spirit that dwells in the once-born is forever opposed to the Spirit that inhabits the heart of the twice-born. This hostility began somewhere in the remote past before the creation of man and continues to this day. The modern effort to bring peace between these two spirits is not only futile but contrary to the moral laws of the universe.

To teach that the spirit of the once-born is at enmity with the Spirit of the twice-born is to bring down upon one's head every kind of violent abuse. No language is too bitter to hurl against the conceited bigot who would dare to draw such a line of distinction between men. Such malignant ideas are at odds with the brotherhood of man, says the once-born, and are held only by the apostles of disunity and hate. This mighty rage against the twice-born only serves to confirm the truth they teach. But this no one seems to notice.

What we need to restore power to the Christian testimony is not soft talk about brotherhood but an honest recognition that two human races occupy the earth simultaneously: a fallen race that sprang from the loins of Adam and a regenerate race that is born of the Spirit through the redemption which is in Christ Jesus.

To accept this truth requires a tough-mindedness and a spiritual maturity that modern Christians simply do not possess. To face up to it hardly contributes to that "peace of mind" after which our religious weaklings bleat so plaintively.

For myself, I long ago decided that I would rather know the truth than be happy in ignorance. I cannot have both truth and happiness, give me truth. We'll have a long time to be happy in heaven.

On the Origin and Nature of Things

The Celebrated Prayer of the great German astronomer, Kepler, has been a benediction to many: "O God, I thank Thee that Thou hast permitted me to think Thy thoughts after Thee."

This prayer is theologically sound because it acknowledges the priority of God in the universe. "In the beginning God" is undoubtedly the most important sentence in the Bible. It is in God that all things begin, and all thoughts as well. In the words of Augustine:

> But Thou, O Lord, who ever livest, and in whom nothing dies, since before the world was, and, indeed, before all that can be called "before," Thou existest, and art the God and Lord of all creatures; and with Thee fixedly abide the causes of all unstable things and the changing sources of all things changeable, and the eternal reasons of all things reasoning and temporal.

Whatever new thing anyone discovers is already old, for it is but the present expression of a previous thought of God. The idea of the thing precedes the thing itself; and when things raise thoughts in the thinker's mind these are the ancient thoughts of God, however imperfectly understood.

When a true thought enters any man's mind, be he saint or sinner, it must of necessity be God's thought, for God is the origin of all true thoughts and things. That is why many real truths are spoken and written by persons other than Christians. Should an atheist, for instance, state that two times two equals four, he would be stating a truth and thinking God's thought after Him, even though he might deny that God exists at all.

In their search for facts men have confused truths with truth. The words of Christ, "Ye shall know the truth, and the truth shall make you free" have been wrenched from their context and used to stir people to the pursuit of knowledge of many kinds with the expectation of being made "free" (John 8:32), by knowledge. Certainly this is not what Christ had in mind when He uttered the words.

Such truths as men discover in the earth beneath and in the astronomic heavens above are properly not truths but facts. We call them truths, as I do here, but they are no more than parts of the jigsaw puzzle of the universe, and when correctly fitted together they provide at least a hint of what the vaster picture is like. But I repeat: They are not truth, and more important, they are not *the truth*. Were every missing piece discovered and laid in place we would still not have the truth, for the truth is not a composite of thoughts and things. The truth should be spelled with a capital *T*, for it is nothing less than the Son of God, the Second Person of the blessed Godhead.

The human mind requires an answer to the question concerning the origin and nature of things. The world as we find it must be accounted for in some way. Philosophers and scientists have sought to account for it, the one by speculation, the other by observation, and in their labors they have come upon many useful and inspiring facts. But they have not found the final Truth. That comes by revelation and illumination.

They who believe the Christian revelation know that the universe is a creation. It is not eternal, since it had a beginning, and it is not the result of a succession of happy coincidences whereby an all but infinite number of matching parts accidentally found each other, fell into place and began to hum. So to believe would require a degree of credulity few persons possess. "I had rather believe all the fables in the Legend, and the Talmud, and the Alcoram," said Bacon, "than that this universe frame is without mind. And therefore God never wrought miracles to convince atheism, because His ordinary works convince it."

Those who have faith are not thrown back upon speculation for the secret of the universe. Faith is an organ of knowledge. "Through faith we understand that the worlds were framed by the word of God, so that things which are seen were not made of things which do appear" (Hebrews 11:3). The voice of Eternal Wisdom declares, "In the beginning God created" and "In the beginning was the Word. . . . All things were made by him; and without him was not any thing made that was made" (Genesis 1:1; John 1:1, 3).

All things came out of the Word, which in the New Testament means the thought and will of God in active expression and is identified with our Lord Jesus Christ. It is the Son who is the Truth that makes men free. Not facts, not scientific knowledge, but eternal Truth delivers men, and that eternal Truth became flesh to dwell among us. "This is life eternal, that they might know thee the only true God, and Jesus Christ, whom thou hast sent" (John 17:3).

Not only the origin of things is revealed, but the nature of things as well. Because the origin of all things is spirit, all things are at bottom spiritual also. This is a moral universe; it is governed by moral laws and will be judged by moral laws at last. Man above all creatures possesses moral perception and is answerable to the spiritual laws that pervade and sustain the world. Pure materialism—that is, the doctrine that matter is the primordial constituent of the universe—is not natural to the human mind. It requires a chronic violation of our basic instincts to accept it as an explanation of the nature of things. And Paul tells us in the first two chapters of his epistle to the Romans how men get into a state of mind to accept such falsehood.

CHAPTER

6

Why People Find
the Bible Difficult

That many persons find the Bible hard to understand will not be denied by those acquainted with the facts. Testimony to the difficulties encountered in Bible reading is too full and too widespread to be dismissed lightly.

In human experience there is usually a complex of causes rather than but one cause for everything, and so it is with the difficulty we run into with the Bible. To the question, Why is the Bible hard to understand? no snap answer can be given; the pert answer is sure to be the wrong one. The problem is multiple instead of singular, and for this reason the efforts to find a single solution to it will be disappointing.

In spite of this I venture to give a short answer to the question, and while it is not the whole answer it is a major one and probably contains within itself most of the answers to what must be an involved and highly complex question. *I believe that we find the Bible difficult because we try to read it as we would read any other book, and it is not the same as any other book.*

The Bible is not addressed to just anybody. Its message is directed to a chosen few. Whether these few are chosen by God in a sovereign act of election or are chosen because they meet certain qualifying conditions, I leave to each one to decide as he may, knowing full well that his decision will be determined by his basic beliefs about such matters as predestination, free will, the eternal decrees and other related doctrines. But whatever may have taken place in eternity, it is obvious what happens in time: Some believe and some do not. It is to those who do and are and have that the Bible is addressed. Those who do not and are not and have not will read it in vain.

Right here I expect some readers to enter strenuous objections, and for reasons not hard to find. Christianity today is man-centered, not God-centered. God is made to wait patiently, even respectfully, on the whims of men. The image of God currently popular is that of a distracted Father, struggling in heartbroken desperation to get people to accept a Savior of whom they feel no need and in whom they have very little interest. To persuade these self-sufficient souls to respond to His generous offers God will do almost anything, even using salesmanship methods and talking down to them in the chummiest way imaginable. This

view of things is, of course, a kind of religious roman-
ticism which, while it often uses flattering and sometimes embarrassing terms in praise of God, manages
nevertheless to make man the star of the show.

The notion that the Bible is addressed to every-
body has wrought confusion within and without
the Church. The effort to apply the teaching of the
Sermon on the Mount to the unregenerate nations
of the world is one example of this. Courts of law
and the military powers of the earth are urged to
follow the teachings of Christ, an obviously impossible thing for them to do. To quote the words of
Christ as guides for policemen, judges and generals
is to misunderstand those words completely and to
reveal a total lack of understanding of the purposes
of divine revelation. The gracious words of Christ
are for the sons and daughters of grace, not for the
Gentile nations whose chosen symbols are the lion,
the eagle, the dragon and the bear.

Not only does God address His words of truth
to those who are able to receive them, He actually
conceals their meaning from those who are not.
The preacher uses stories to make truth clear; our
Lord often used them to obscure it. The parables
of Christ were the exact opposite to the modern
"illustration," which is meant to give light; the
parables were "dark sayings," and Christ asserted
that He sometimes used them so that His disciples
could understand and His enemies could not.
(See Matthew 13:10-17.) As the pillar of fire gave
light to Israel but was cloud and darkness to the
Egyptians, so our Lord's words shine in the hearts

of His people but leave the self-confident unbeliever in the obscurity of moral night. The saving power of the Word is reserved for those for whom it is intended. The secret of the Lord is with them that fear Him. The impenitent heart will find the Bible but a skeleton of facts without flesh or life or breath. Shakespeare may be enjoyed without penitence; we may understand Plato without believing a word he says; but penitence and humility along with faith and obedience are necessary to a right understanding of the Scriptures.

In natural matters faith follows evidence and is impossible without it, but in the realm of the spirit faith precedes understanding; it does not follow it. The natural man must know in order to believe; the spiritual man must believe in order to know. The faith that saves is not a conclusion drawn from evidence; it is a moral thing of the spirit, a supernatural infusion of confidence in Jesus Christ, a very gift of God.

The faith that saves reposes in the Person of Christ; it leads at once to a committal of the total being to Christ, an act impossible to the natural man. To believe rightly is as much a miracle as was the coming forth of dead Lazarus at the command of Christ.

The Bible is a supernatural book and can be understood only by supernatural aid.

Faith: The Misunderstood Doctrine

I n the divine scheme of salvation the doctrine of faith is central. God addresses His words to faith, and where no faith is no true revelation is possible. "Without faith it is impossible to please him" (Hebrews 11:6).

Every benefit flowing from the atonement of Christ comes to the individual through the gateway of faith. Forgiveness, cleansing, regeneration, the Holy Spirit, all answers to prayer, are given to faith and received by faith. There is no other way. This is common evangelical doctrine and is accepted wherever the cross of Christ is understood.

Because faith is so vital to all our hopes, so necessary to the fulfillment of our hearts, we dare take nothing for granted concerning it. Anything that carries with it so much of weal or woe, which indeed decides our heaven or our hell, is too important to neglect. We simply must not allow ourselves to be uninformed or misinformed. We must know.

For a number of years my heart has been troubled over the doctrine of faith as it is received and taught among evangelical Christians everywhere. Great emphasis is laid upon faith in orthodox circles, and that is good; but still I am troubled. Specifically, my fear is that the modern conception of faith is not the biblical one; that when the teachers of our day use the word they do no mean what Bible writers meant when they used it.

The causes of my uneasiness are these:

1. The lack of spiritual fruit in the lives of so many who claim to have faith.
2. The rarity of a radical change in the conduct and general outlook of persons professing their new faith in Christ as their personal Savior.
3. The failure of teachers to define or even describe the thing to which the word faith is supposed to refer.
4. The heartbreaking failure of multitudes of seekers, be they ever so earnest, to make anything out of the doctrine or to receive any satisfying experience through it.
5. The real danger that a doctrine that is parroted so widely and received so uncritically by so many is false as understood by them.
6. I have seen faith put forward as a substitute for obedience, an escape from reality, a refuge from the necessity of hard thinking, a hiding

place for weak character. I have known people to miscall by the name of faith high animal spirits, natural optimism, emotional thrills and nervous tics.

7. Plain horse sense ought to tell us that anything that makes no change in the man who professes it makes no difference to God either, and it is an easily observable fact that for countless numbers of persons the change from no-faith to faith makes no actual difference in life.

Perhaps it will help us to know what faith is if we first notice what it is not. It is not the believing of a statement we know to be true. The human mind is so constructed that it must of necessity believe when the evidence presented to it is convincing. It cannot help itself. When the evidence fails to convince, no faith is possible. No threats, no punishment can compel the mind to believe against clear evidence.

Faith based upon reason is faith of a kind, it is true; *but it is not of the character of Bible faith,* for it follows the evidence infallibly and has nothing of a moral or spiritual nature in it. Neither can the absence of faith based upon reason be held against anyone, for the evidence, not the individual, decides the verdict. To send a man to hell whose only crime was to follow evidence straight to its proper conclusion would be palpable injustice; to justify a sinner on the grounds that he had made up his mind according to the plain facts would be to make salvation the result of workings of a common law of the mind as applicable to Judas as to Paul. It would take salvation out of the realm of the volitional and place it in the mental, where according to the Scriptures, it surely does not belong.

True faith rests upon the character of God and asks no further proof than the moral perfections of the One who cannot lie. It is enough that God said it, and if the statement should contradict every one of the five senses and all the conclusions of logic as well, still the believer continues to believe. "Let God be true, but every man a liar" (Romans 3:4), is the language of true faith. Heaven approves such faith because it rises above mere proofs and rests in the bosom of God.

In recent years among certain evangelicals there has arisen a movement designed to prove the truths of Scriptures by appeal to science. Evidence is sought in the natural world to support supernatural revelation. Snowflakes, blood, stones, strange marine creatures, birds and many other natural objects are brought forward as proof that the Bible is true. This is touted as being a great support to faith, the idea being that if a Bible doctrine can be *proved* to be true, faith will spring up and flourish as a consequence.

What these brethren do not see is that the very fact that they feel a necessity to seek proof for the truths of the Scriptures proves something else altogether, namely, their own basic unbelief. When God speaks unbelief asks, "How shall I know that this is true?" I AM THAT I AM is the only grounds for faith. To dig among the rocks or search under the sea for evidence to support Scriptures is to insult the One who wrote them. Certainly I do not believe that this is done intentionally; but I cannot see how we can escape the conclusion that it is done, nevertheless.

Faith as the Bible knows it is confidence in God and His Son Jesus Christ; it is the response of the soul to the divine character as revealed in the Scriptures; and even this response is impossible apart from the prior inworking of the Holy Spirit. Faith is a gift of God to a penitent soul and has nothing whatsoever to do with the senses or the data they afford. Faith is a miracle; it is the ability God gives to trust His Son, and anything that does not result in action in accord with the will of God is not faith but something else short of it.

Faith and morals are two sides of the same coin. Indeed the very essence of faith is moral. Any professed faith in Christ as personal Savior that does not bring the life under plenary obedience to Christ as Lord is inadequate and must betray its victim at the last.

The man who believes will obey; failure to obey is convincing proof that there is not true faith present. To attempt the impossible, God must give faith or there will be none, and He gives faith to the obedient heart only. Where real repentance is, there is obedience; for repentance is not only sorrow for past failures and sins, it is a determination to begin now to do the will of God as He reveals it to us.

True Religion Is Not
Feeling but Willing

One of the puzzling questions likely to turn up sooner or later to vex the seeking Christian is how he can fulfill the scriptural command to love God with all his heart and his neighbor as himself.

The earnest Christian, as he meditates on his sacred obligation to love God and mankind, may experience a sense of frustration gendered by the knowledge that he just cannot seem to work up any emotional thrill over his Lord or his brothers. He wants to, but he cannot. The delightful wells of feeling simply will not flow.

Many honest persons have become discouraged by the absence of religious emotion and concluded that they are not really Christian after all. They conclude that they must have missed the way somewhere back there and their religion is little more than an empty profession. So for a while they belabor themselves for their coldness and finally settle into a state of dull discouragement, hardly knowing what to think. They do believe in God; they do indeed trust Christ as their Savior, but the love they hoped to feel consistently eludes them. What is the trouble?

The problem is not a light one. A real difficulty is involved, one which may be stated in the form of a question: How can I love by command? Of all the emotions of which the soul is capable, love is by far the freest, the most unreasoning, the one least likely to spring up at the call of duty or obligation and surely the one that will not come at the command of another. No law has ever been passed that can compel one moral being to love another, for by the very nature of it love must be voluntary. No one can be coerced or frightened into loving anyone. Love just does not come that way. So what are we to do with our Lord's command to love God and our neighbor?

To find our way out of the shadows and into the cheerful sunlight we need only to know that there are two kinds of love: the love of *feeling* and the love of *willing*. The one lies in the emotions, the other in the will. Over the one we may have little control. It comes and goes, rises and falls, flares up and disappears as it chooses, and changes from hot to warm to cool and back to warm again very much as does the weather. Such love was not in the mind of Christ when He told His people to love God and each other. As well command a butterfly to light on our shoulder as to attempt to command this whimsical kind of affection to visit our hearts. The love the Bible enjoins is not the love of feeling; *it is the love of willing, the willed tendency of the heart.* (For these two happy phrases I am indebted to another, a master of the inner life whose pen was only a short time ago stilled by death.)

God never intended that such a being as man should be the plaything of his feelings. The emotional life is a proper and noble part of the total personality, but it is, by its very nature, of secondary importance. *Religion lies in the will, and so does righteousness.* The only good that God recognizes is a willed good; the only valid holiness is a willed holiness.

It should be a cheering thought that before God every man is what he wills to be. The first requirement in conversion is a rectified will. "If any man will," says our Lord, and leaves it there. To meet the requirements of love toward God the soul need but will to love and the miracle begins to blossom like the budding of Aaron's rod.

The will is the automatic pilot that keeps the soul on course. "Flying is easy," said a friend who flies his own plane. "Just take her up, point her in the direction you want her to go and set the pilot. After that she'll fly herself." While we must not press the figure too far, it is yet blessedly true that the will, not the feelings, determines moral direction.

The root of all evil in human nature is the corruption of the will. The thoughts and intents of the heart are wrong and as a consequence the whole life is wrong. Repentance is primarily a change of moral purpose, a sudden and often violent reversal of the soul's direction. The prodigal son took his first step upward from the pigsty when he said, "I will arise and go to my father" (Luke 15:18). As he had once willed to leave his father's house, now he willed to return. His subsequent action proved his expressed purpose to be sincere. He did return.

Someone may infer from the above that we are ruling out the joy of the Lord as a valid part of the Christian life. While no one who reads these columns regularly would be likely to draw such erroneous conclusion, a chance reader might be led astray; a further word of explanation is therefore indicated:

To love God with all our heart we must first of all *will* to do so. We should repent our lack of love and determine from this moment on to make God the object of our devotion. We should set our affections on things above and aim our hearts toward Christ and heavenly things. We should read the Scriptures devotionally every day and prayerfully obey them, always firmly *willing* to love God with all our heart and our neighbor as ourself.

If we do these things we may be sure that we shall experience a wonderful change in our whole inward life. We shall soon find to our great delight that our feelings are becoming less erratic and are beginning to move in the direction of the "willed tendency of the heart." Our emotions will become disciplined and directed. We shall begin to taste the "piercing sweetness" of the love of Christ. Our religious affection will begin to mount evenly on steady wings instead of flitting about idly without purpose or intelligent direction. The whole life, like a delicate instrument, will be tuned to sing the praises of Him who loved us and washed us from our sins in His own blood.

But first of all we must will, for the will is master of the heart.

How to Make
Spiritual Progress

The complacency of Christians is the scandal of Christianity.

Time is short, and eternity is long. The end of all things is at hand. Man has proved himself morally unfit to manage the world in which he has been placed by the kindness of the Almighty. He has jockeyed himself to the edge of the crater and cannot go back, and in terrible fear he is holding his breath against the awful moment when he will be plunged into the inferno.

In the meantime, a company of people exist on the earth who claim to have the answer to all life's major questions. They claim to have found the way back to God, release from their sins, life everlasting and a sure guarantee of heaven in the world to come.

These are the Christians. They declare that Jesus Christ is very God of very God, made flesh to dwell among us. They insist that He is the Way, the Truth and the Life. They testify that He is to them Wisdom, Righteousness, Sanctification and Redemption, and they steadfastly assert that He will be to them the Resurrection and the Life for eternity to come.

These Christians know, and when pressed will admit, that their finite hearts have explored but a pitifully small part of the infinite riches that are theirs in Christ Jesus. They read the lives of the great saints whose fervent desire after God carried them far up the mountain toward spiritual perfection, and for a brief moment they may yearn to be like these fiery souls whose light and fragrance still linger in the world where they once lived and labored. But the longing soon passes. The world is too much with them and the claims of their earthly lives are too insistent; so they settle back to live their ordinary lives and accept the customary as normal. After a while they manage to achieve some kind of inner content and that is the last we hear of them.

This contentment with inadequate and imperfect progress in the life of holiness is, I repeat, a scandal in the Church of the First-born. The whole weight of Scripture is against such a thing. The Holy Spirit constantly seeks to arouse the complacent. "Let us go on" is the word of the Spirit. The apostle Paul embodies this in his noble testimony as found in his Philippian epistle:

But what things were gain to me, those I counted loss for Christ. Yea doubtless, and I count all things but loss for the excellency of the knowledge of Christ Jesus my Lord: for whom I have suffered the loss of all things, and do count them but dung, that I may win Christ, . . . that I may know him, and the power of his resurrection. . . . But this one thing I do, forgetting those things which are behind, and reaching forth unto those things which are before, I press toward the mark for the prize of the high calling of God in Christ Jesus. (3:7-8, 10, 13-14)

If we accept this as the sincere expression of a normal Christian I do not see how we can justify our own indifference toward spiritual things. But should someone feel a desire to make definite progress in the life of Christ, what can he do to get on with it? Here are a few suggestions:

1. *Strive to get beyond mere pensive longing.* Set your face like a flint and begin to put your life in order. Every man is as holy as he really wants to be. But the want must be all-compelling.

   Tie up the loose ends of your life. Begin to tithe; institute family prayer; pay up your debts as far as possible and make some kind of frank arrangement with every creditor you cannot pay immediately; make restitution as far as you can; set aside time to pray and search the Scriptures; surrender wholly to the will of God. You will be surprised and delighted with the results.

2. *Put away every un-Christian habit from you.* If other Christians practice it without compunction, God may be calling you to come nearer to Him than these other Christians care to come. Remember the words, "Others may, you cannot." Do not condemn or criticize, but seek a better way. God will honor you.

3. *Get Christ Himself in the focus of your heart and keep Him there continually.* Only in Christ will you find complete fulfillment. In Him you may be united to the Godhead in conscious, vital awareness. Remember that all of God is accessible to you through Christ. Cultivate His knowledge above everything else on earth.

4. *Throw your heart open to the Holy Spirit and invite Him to fill you.* He will do it. Let no one interpret the Scriptures for you in such a way as to rule out the Father's gift of the Spirit. Every man is as full of the Spirit as he wants to be. Make your heart a vacuum and the Spirit will rush into fill it.

   Nowhere in the Scriptures nor in Christian biography was anyone ever filled with the Spirit who did not know that he had been, and nowhere was anyone filled who did not know when. And no one was ever filled gradually.

5. *Be hard on yourself and easy on others.* Carry your own cross but never lay one on the back of another. Begin to practice the presence of God. Cultivate the fellowship of the Triune God by prayer, humility, obedience and self-abnegation.

   Let any Christian do these things and he will make rapid spiritual progress. There is every reason why we should all go forward in our Christian lives and no reason why we should not. Let us go on.

This chapter was written for the Gideons, Int., in Toronto, and used by their permission.

10

The Old Cross and the New

All unannounced and mostly undetected there has come in modern times a new cross into popular evangelical circles. It is like the old cross, but different: the likenesses are superficial; the differences, fundamental.

From this new cross has sprung a new philosophy of the Christian life, and from that new philosophy has come a new evangelical technique—a new type of meeting and a new kind of preaching. This new evangelism employs the same language as the old, but its content is not the same and its emphasis not as before.

The old cross would have no truck with the world. For Adam's proud flesh it meant the end of the journey. It carried into effect the sentence imposed by the law of Sinai. The new cross is not opposed to the human race; rather, it is a friendly pal and, if understood aright, it is the source of oceans of good clean fun and innocent enjoyment. It lets Adam live without interference. His life motivation is unchanged; he still lives for his own pleasure, only now he takes delight in singing choruses and watching religious movies instead of singing bawdy songs and drinking hard liquor. The accent is still on enjoyment, though the fun is now on a higher place morally if not intellectually.

The new cross encourages a new entirely different evangelistic approach. The evangelist does not demand abnegation of the old life before a new life can be received. He preaches not contrasts but similarities. He seeks to key into public interest by showing that Christianity makes no unpleasant demands; rather, it offers the same thing the world does, only on a higher level. Whatever the sin-mad world happens to be clamoring after at the moment is cleverly shown to be the very thing the gospel offers, only the religious product is better.

The new cross does not slay the sinner; it redirects him. It gears him into a cleaner and jollier way of living and saves his self-respect. To the self-assertive it says, "Come and assert yourself for Christ." To the egotist it says, "Come and do your boasting in the Lord." To the thrill seeker it says, "Come and enjoy the thrill of Christian fellowship." The Christian message is slanted in the direction of the current vogue in order to make it acceptable to the public.

The philosophy back of this kind of thing may be sincere but its sincerity does not save it from being false. It is false because it is blind. It misses completely the whole meaning of the cross.

The old cross is a symbol of death. It stands for the abrupt, violent end of a human being. The man in Roman times who took up his cross and started down the road had already said good-bye to his friends. He was not coming back. He was going out to have it ended. The cross made no compromise, modified nothing, spared nothing; it slew all of the man, completely and for good. It did not try to keep on good terms with its victim. It struck cruel and hard, and when it had finished its work, the man was no more.

The race of Adam is under death sentence. There is no commutation and no escape. God cannot approve any of the fruits of sin, however innocent they may appear or beautiful to the eyes of men. God salvages the individual by liquidating him and then raising him again to newness of life.

That evangelism which draws friendly parallels between the ways of God and the ways of men is false to the Bible and cruel to the souls of its hearers. The faith of Christ does not parallel the world; it intersects it. In coming to Christ we do not bring our old life up onto a higher place; we leave it at the cross. The corn of wheat must fall into the ground and die.

We who preach the gospel must not think of ourselves as public relations agents sent to establish good will between Christ and the world. We must not imagine ourselves commissioned to make Christ acceptable to big business, the press, the world of sports or modern education. We are not diplomats but prophets, and our message is not a compromise but an ultimatum.

God offers life, but not an improved old life. The life He offers is life out of death. It stands always on the far side of the cross. Whoever would possess it must pass under the rod. He must repudiate himself and concur in God's just sentence against him.

What does this mean to the individual, the condemned man who would find life in Christ Jesus? How can this theology be translated into life? Simply, he must repent and believe. He must forsake his sins and then go on to forsake himself. Let him cover nothing, defend nothing, excuse nothing. Let him not seek to make terms with God, but let him bow his head before the stroke of God's stern displeasures and acknowledge himself worthy to die.

Having done this let him gaze with simple trust upon the risen Savior, and from Him will come life and rebirth and cleansing and power. The cross that ended the earthly life of Jesus now puts an end to the sinner; and the power that raised Christ from the dead now raises him to a new life along with Christ.

To any who may object to this or count it merely a narrow and private view of truth, let me say God has set His hallmark of approval upon this message from Paul's day to the present. Whether stated in these exact words or not, this has been the content of all preaching that has brought life and power to the world through the centuries. The mystics, the reformers, the revivalists have put their emphasis here, and signs and wonders and mighty operations of the Holy Ghost gave witness to God's approval.

Dare we, the heirs of such a legacy of power, tamper with the truth? Dare we with our stubby pencils erase the lines of the blueprint or alter the pattern shown us in the Mount? May God forbid. Let us preach the old cross and we will know the old power.

There Is No Wisdom in Sin

The world has divided men into two classes, the stupid good people and the clever wicked ones.

This false classification runs through much of the literature of the last centuries from the classics to the comic strip, from Shakespeare's Polonius, who furnished his son with a set of good but dull moral platitudes, to Camp's Li'l Abner, who would never knowingly do a wrong act but who would rather fall on his head than on his feet because there is more feeling in his feet than in his head.

In the Holy Scriptures things are quite the opposite. There righteousness is always associated with wisdom and evil with folly. Whatever other factors may be present in an act of wrongdoing, folly is one that is never absent. To do a wrong act a man must for the moment think wrong; he must exercise bad judgment.

If this is true then the devil is creation's prime
fool, for when he gambled on his ability to unseat
the Almighty he was guilty of an act of judgment so
bad as to be imbecilic. He is said to have had a great
amount of wisdom, but his wisdom must have de-
serted him at the time of his first sin, for surely he
grossly underestimated the power of God and as
grossly overestimated his own. The devil is not now
pictured in the Scriptures as wise, only as shrewd.
We are warned not against his wisdom but against
his wiles, something very different.

Sin, I repeat, in addition to anything else it may
be, is always an act of wrong judgment. To com-
mit a sin a man must for the moment believe that
things are different from what they really are; he
must confound values; he must see the moral universe out of focus; he must accept a lie as truth
and see truth as a lie; he must ignore the signs on
the highway and drive with his eyes shut; he
must act as if he had no soul and was not accountable for his moral choices.

Sin is never a thing to be proud of. No act is wise
that ignores remote consequences, and sin always
does. Sin sees only today, or at most tomorrow;
never the day after tomorrow, next month or next
year. Death and judgment are pushed aside as if
they did not exist and the sinner becomes for the
time a practical atheist who by his act denies not
only the existence of God but the concept of life after death.

History is replete with examples of men whose
intellectual powers were great but whose practi-

cal judgment was almost nil: Einstein, for instance, who was a mathematical genius but who
could not look after his own bank account and
who absent-mindedly ran his little motorboat
aground with the excuse that he "must have been
thinking about something else." We can smile at
this, but there is nothing humorous about that
other class of men who had brilliant minds but
whose moral judgment was sadly awry. To this
class belong such men as Lucretius, Voltaire, Shel-
ley, Oscar Wilde, Walt Whitman and thousands
of others whose names are less widely known.

The notion that the careless sinner is the smart
fellow and the serious-minded Christian, though
well-intentioned, is a stupid dolt altogether out of
touch with life will not stand up under scrutiny.
Sin is basically an act of moral folly, and the
greater the folly the greater the fool.

It is time the young people of this generation
learned that there is nothing smart about wrongdoing and nothing stupid about righteousness. We
must stop negotiating with evil. We Christians must
stop apologizing for our moral position and start
making our voices heard, exposing sin for the enemy of the human race which it surely is and setting
forth righteousness and true holiness as the only
worthy pursuits for moral beings.

The idea that sin is modern is false. There has not
been a new sin invented since the beginning of re-
corded history. That new vice that breaks out to
horrify decent citizens and worry the police is not
really new. Flip open that book written centuries

ago and you will find it described there. The reckless sinner trying to think of some new way to express his love of iniquity can do no more than imitate others like himself, now long dead. He is not the bright rebel he fancies himself to be but a weak and stupid fellow who must follow along in the long parade of death toward the point of no return.

If the hoary head is a crown of glory when it is found in the way of righteousness, it is a fool's cap when it is found in the way of sin. An old sinner is an awesome and frightening spectacle. One feels about him much as one feels about the condemned man on his way to the gallows. A sense of numb terror and shock fills the heart. The knowledge that the condemned man was once a red-checked boy only heightens the feeling, and the knowledge that the aged rebel now beyond reclamation once went up to the house of God on a Sunday morning to the sweet sound of church bells makes even the trusting Christian humble and a little bit scared. There but for the grace of God goes he.

I am among those who believe that our Western civilization is on its way to perishing. It has many commendable qualities, most of which it has borrowed from the Christian ethic, but it lacks the element of moral wisdom that would give it permanence. Future historians will record that we of the twentieth century had intelligence enough to create a great civilization but not the moral wisdom to preserve it.

Three Degrees of Religious Knowledge

In our knowledge of divine things three degrees may be distinguished: the knowledge furnished by reason, by faith and by spiritual experience respectively. These three degrees of knowledge correspond to the departments of the tabernacle in the ancient Levitical order: the outer court, the holy place and the holy of holies.

Far in, beyond the "second veil," was the holiest of all, having as its lone piece of furniture the Ark of the Covenant with the cherubim of glory shadowing the mercy seat. There between the outstretched wings dwelt in awesome splendor the fire of God's presence, the Shekinah. No light of nature reached that sacred place, only the pure radiance of Him who is light and in whom there is no darkness at all. To that solemn Presence no one could approach except the high priest once each year with blood of atonement.

Farther out, and separated by a heavy veil, was the holy place, a sacred place indeed but removed from the Presence and always accessible to the priests of Israel. Here also the light of sun and moon was excluded; light was furnished by the shining of the seven golden candlesticks.

The court of the priests was out farther still, a large enclosure in which were the brazen altar and the lavar. This was open to the sky and received the normal light of nature.

All was of God and all was divine, but the quality of the worshiper's knowledge became surer and more sublime as he moved in from the outer court toward the mercy seat and the Presence, where at last he was permitted to gaze upon the cherubim of glory and the deep burning Fire that glowed between their outstretched wings.

All this illustrates if it does not typify the three degrees of knowledge possible to a Christian. It is not proper that we should press every detail in an effort to find in the beautiful Old Testament picture more than is actually there; but the most cautious expositor could hardly object to our using the earthly and external to throw into relief the internal and the heavenly.

Nature is a great teacher and at her feet we may learn much that is good and ennobling. The Bible itself teaches this: "The heavens declare the glory of God; and the firmament sheweth his handywork. Day unto day uttereth speech, and night unto night sheweth knowledge" (Psalm 19:1-2). "Go to the ant, thou sluggard; consider her ways, and be wise" (Proverbs 6:6). "Behold the fowls of the air" (Matthew 6:26). "For the invisible things of him from the creation of the world are clearly seen, being understood by the things that are made, even his eternal power and Godhead" (Romans 1:20). Reason working on data furnished by observation of natural objects tells us a lot about God and spiritual things. This is too obvious to require proof. Everyone knows it.

But there is knowledge beyond and above that furnished by observation; it is knowledge received by faith. "In religion faith plays the part by experience in the things of the world." Divine revelation through the inspired Scriptures offers data which lie altogether outside of and above the power of the mind to discover. The mind can make its deductions after it has received these data by faith, but it cannot find them by itself. No technique is known to man by which he can learn, for instance, that God in the beginning created the heaven and the earth or that there are three Persons in the Godhead; that God is love or that Christ died for sinners or that He now sits at the right hand of the Majesty in the heavens. If we ever come to know these things it must be by receiving as true a body of doctrine which we have no way of verifying. This is the knowledge of faith.

There is yet a purer knowledge than this; it is knowledge by direct spiritual experience. About it there is an immediacy that places it beyond doubt. Since it was not acquired by reason operating on intellectual data, the possibility of error is eliminated. Through the indwelling Spirit the human spirit is brought into immediate contact with higher spiritual reality. It looks upon, tastes, feels and sees the powers of the world to come and has a conscious encounter with God invisible.

Let it be understood that such knowledge is experienced rather than acquired. It does not consist of findings about something; it is the thing itself. It is not a compound of religious truths. It is an element which cannot be separated into parts. One who enjoys this kind of knowledge is able to understand the exhortation in the book of Job: "Acquaint now thyself with him, and be at peace" (22:21). To such a man God is not a conclusion drawn from evidence nor is He the sum of what the Bible teaches about Him. He knows God in the last irreducible meaning of the word *know*. It may almost be said that *God happened to him*.

Maybe Christ said all this more simply in John 14:21: "I . . . will manifest myself to him." For what have we been laboring here but the sublimely simple New Testament teaching that the Triune God wills to dwell in the redeemed man's heart, constantly making His presence known? What on earth or in heaven above can be a greater beatitude?

The Sanctification of the Secular

The New Testament teaches that all things are pure to the pure, and I think we may assume that to the evil man all things are evil. The thing itself is not good or bad; goodness or badness belongs to human personality.

Everything depends upon the state of our interior lives and our heart's relation to God. The man who walks with God will see and know that for him there is no strict line separating the sacred from the secular. He will acknowledge that there lies around him a world of created things that are innocent in themselves; and he will know, too, that there are a thousand human acts that are neither good nor bad except as they may be done by good or bad men. The busy world around us is filled with work, travel, marrying, rearing our young, burying our dead, buying, selling, sleep-

ing, eating and mixing in common social intercourse with our fellowmen.

These activities and all else that goes to fill up our
days are usually separated in our minds from
prayer, church attendance and such specific religious acts as are performed by ministers most of the
week and by laymen briefly once or twice weekly.

Because the vast majority of men engage in the
complicated business of living while trusting
wholly in themselves, without reference to God or
redemption, we Christians have come to call these
common activities "secular" and to attribute to them
at least a degree of evil, an evil which is not inherent
in them and which they do not necessarily possess.

The apostle Paul teaches that every simple act
of our lives may be sacramental. "Whether therefore ye eat, or drink, or whatsoever ye do, do all to
the glory of God" (1 Corinthians 10:31). And
again, "Whatsoever ye do in word or deed, do all
in the name of the Lord Jesus, giving thanks to
God and the Father by him" (Colossians 3:17).

Some of the great saints, who were great because
they took such admonitions seriously and sought to
practice them, managed to achieve the sanctification of the secular, or perhaps I should say the aboli-
tion of the secular. Their attitude toward life's
common things raised those above the common
and imparted to them an aura of divinity. These
pure souls broke down the high walls that separated the various areas of their lives from each other
and saw all as one; and that one they offered to God
as a holy oblation acceptable to God by Jesus Christ.

Nicholas Herman (Brother Lawrence) made his most common act one of devotion: "The time of business does not with me differ from the time of prayer," he said, "and in the noise and clatter of my kitchen, while several persons are at the same time calling for different things, I possess God in as great tranquility as if I were upon my knees at the blessed sacrament."

Francis of Assisi accepted the whole creation as his house of worship and called upon everything great and small to join him in adoration of the Godhead. Mother earth, the burning sun, the silver moon, the stars of evening, wind, water, flowers, fruits—all were invited to praise with him their God and King. Hardly a spot was left that could be called secular. The whole world glowed like Moses' bush with the light of God, and before it the saint kneeled and removed his shoes. Thomas Traherne, the seventeenth-century Christian writer, declared that the children of the King can never enjoy the world aright till every morning they wake up in heaven, see themselves in the Father's palace and look upon the skies, the earth and the air as celestial joys, having such a reverent esteem for all as if they were among the angels.

All this is not to ignore the Fall of man nor to deny the presence of sin in the world. No believing man can deny the Fall, as no observing man can deny the reality of sin; and as far as I know no responsible thinker has ever held that sin could ever be made other than sinful, whether by prayer or faith or spiritual ministrations. Neither the inspired writers of Holy Scripture nor those illuminated souls who have based their teachings upon those Scriptures have tried to make sin other than exceedingly sinful. It is possible to recognize the sacredness of all things even while admitting that for the time the mystery of sin worketh in the children of disobedience and the whole creation groaneth and travaileth, waiting for the manifestation of the children of God.

Traherne saw the apparent contradiction and explained it:

> To contemn the world and to enjoy the world are things contrary to each other. How can we contemn the world, which we are born to enjoy? Truly there are two worlds. One was made by God, and the other by men. That made by God was great and beautiful. Before the Fall it was Adam's joy and the temple of his glory. That made by men is a Babel of confusions: invented riches, pomps and vanities, brought in by sin. Give all (saith Thomas à Kempis) for all. Leave the one that you may enjoy the other.

Such souls as these achieved the sanctification of the secular. The Church today is suffering from the secularization of the sacred. By accepting the world's values, thinking its thoughts and adopting its ways we have dimmed the glory that shines overhead. We have not been able to bring earth to the judgment of heaven so we have brought heaven to the judgment of the earth. Pity us, Lord, for we know not what we do!

God Must Be
Loved for Himself

God being who He is must always be sought for Himself, never as a means toward something else.

Whoever seeks other objects and not God is on his own; he may obtain those objects if he is able, but he will never have God. God is never found accidentally. "Ye shall seek me, and find me, when ye shall search for me with all your heart" (Jeremiah 29:13).

Whoever seeks God as a means toward desired ends will not find God. The mighty God, the maker of heaven and earth, will not be one of many treasures, not even the chief of all treasures. He will be all in all or He will be nothing. God will not be used. His mercy and grace are infinite and His patient understanding is beyond measure, but He will not aid men in their selfish striving after personal gain. He will not help men to attain ends which, when attained, usurp the place He by every right should hold in their interest and affection.

Yet popular Christianity has as one of its most effective talking points the idea that God exists to help people to get ahead in this world. The God of the poor has become the God of an affluent society. Christ no longer refuses to be a judge or a divider between money-hungry brothers. He can now be persuaded to assist the brother that has accepted Him to get the better of the brother who has not.

A crass example of the modern effort to use God for selfish purposes is the well-known comedian who, after repeated failures, promised someone he called God that if He would help him to make good in the entertainment world he would repay Him by giving generously to the care of sick children. Shortly afterward he hit the big time in the nightclubs and on television. He has kept his word and is raising large sums of money to build children's hospitals. These contributions to charity, he feels, are a small price to pay for a success in one of the sleaziest fields of human endeavor.

One might excuse the act of this entertainer as something to be expected of a twentieth-century pagan; but that multitudes of evangelicals in North America should actually believe that God had anything to do with the whole business is not so easily overlooked. This low and false view of Deity is one major reason for the immense popularity God enjoys these days among well-fed Westerners.

The teaching of the Bible is that God is Himself the end for which man was created. "Whom have I in heaven but thee?" cried the psalmist, "and there is none upon earth that I desire beside thee" (Psalm 73:25). The first and greatest commandment is to love God with every power of our entire being. Where love like that exists there can be no place for a second object. If we love God as much as we should, surely we cannot dream of a loved object beyond Him which He might help us to obtain.

Bernard of Clairvaux begins his radiant little treatise on the love of God with a question and an answer. The question: Why should we love God? The answer: Because He is God. He develops the idea further, but for the enlightened heart little more need be said. We should love God because He is God. Beyond this the angels cannot think.

Being who He is, God is to be loved for His own sake. He is the reason for our loving Him, just as He is the reason for His loving us and for every other act He has performed, is performing and will perform, world without end. God's primary reason for everything is His own good pleasure. The search for secondary reasons is gratuitous and mostly futile. It affords occupation for theologians and adds pages to books on doctrine, but that it ever turns up any true explanations is doubtful.

But it is the nature of God to share. His mighty acts of creation and redemption were done for His good pleasure, but His pleasure extends to all created things. One has but to look at a healthy child at play or listen to the song of a bird at sundown and he will know that God meant His universe to be a joyful one.

Those who have been spiritually enabled to love God for Himself will find a thousand fountains springing up from the rainbow-circled throne and bringing countless treasures which are to be received with reverent thanksgiving as being the overflow of God's love for His children. Each gift is a bonus of grace which because it was not sought for itself may be enjoyed without injury to the soul. These include the simple blessings of life, such as health, a home, a family, congenial friends, food, shelter, the pure joys of nature or the more artificial pleasures of music and art.

The effort to find these treasures by direct search apart from God has been the major activity of mankind through the centuries; and this has been man's burden and man's woe. The effort to gain them as the ulterior motive back of accepting Christ may be something new under the sun; but new or old it is an evil that can only bring judgment at last.

God wills that we should love Him for Himself alone with no hidden reasons, trusting Him to be to us all our natures require. Our Lord said all this much better: "Seek ye first the kingdom of God, and his righteousness; and all these things shall be added unto you" (Matthew 6:33).

True Faith Is Active, Not Passive

Aa Christian is one who believes on Jesus Christ as Lord. With this statement every evangelical agrees. Indeed there would appear to be nothing else to do, since the New Testament is crystal clear about the matter.

This first acknowledgment of Christ as Lord and Savior is usually followed by baptism and membership in a Protestant church, the one because it satisfies a craving for fellowship with others of like mind. A few Christians shy away from organized religion, but the vast majority, while they recognize the imperfections of the churches, nevertheless feel that they can serve their Lord better in the church than out of it.

There is, however, one serious flaw in all this: It is that many—would I overstate the case if I said the majority?—of those who confess their faith in Christ and enter into association with the community of believers have little joy in their hearts, no peace in their minds and from all external appearances are no better morally than the ordinary educated citizen who takes no interest whatever in religion and, of course, makes no profession of Christianity. Why is this?

I believe it is the result of an inadequate concept of Christianity and an imperfect understanding of the revolutionary character of Christian discipleship. Certainly there is nothing new in my conclusion. The evangelists are loud in their lamentation over the bodies of dead church members, as well they might be, and many thoughtful articles and books appear from time to time dealing with the serious hiatus between faith and practice among Christians.

Why then add another feeble voice to the many? Because many who lament the condition do not seem to know what to do about it, and because I believe that the way is plain, if hard; and that there is no excuse for going on at this poor dying rate when we can enjoy abundant life in Christ Jesus. True faith brings a spiritual and moral transformation and an inward witness that cannot be mistaken. These come when we stop believing in belief and start believing in the Lord Jesus Christ indeed.

True faith is not passive but active. It requires that we meet certain conditions, that we allow the teachings of Christ to dominate our total lives from the moment we believe. The man of saving faith must be willing to be different from others. The effort to enjoy the benefits of redemption while enmeshed in the world is futile. We must choose one or the other; and faith quickly makes its choice, one from which there is no retreat.

The change experienced by a truly converted man is equal to that of a man moving to another country. The regenerated soul feels no more at home in the world than Abraham felt when he left Ur of the Chaldees and set out for the land of promise. Apart from his own small company he was a stranger to everyone around him. He was called "Abraham the Hebrew," and if he spoke the language of the people among whom he took up his dwelling place, he spoke it with an accent. They all knew that he was not one of them.

This journey from Ur to Bethel is taken by every soul that sets out to follow Christ. It is, however, not a journey for the feet but for the heart. The newborn Christian is a migrant; he has come into the kingdom of God from his old home in the kingdom of man and he must get set for the violent changes that will inevitably follow.

One of the first changes will be a shift of interest from earth to heaven, from men to God, from time to eternity, from earthly gain to Christ and His eternal kingdom. Suddenly, or slowly but surely, he will develop a new pattern of life. Old things will pass away and behold, all things will become new, first inwardly and then outwardly; for the change within him will soon begin to express itself by corresponding changes in his manner of living.

The transformation will show itself in many ways and his former friends will begin to worry about him. At first they will tease him and then chide him; and if he persists in his determination to follow Christ they may begin to oppose and persecute. The once-born never understand the twice-born, and still after thousands of years Cain hates Abel and Esau threatens Jacob. It is as true today as it was in Bible times that the man who hates his sins too much will get into trouble with those who do not hate sin enough. People resent having their friends turn away from them and by implication condemn their way of life.

The change will reveal itself further in what the new Christian reads, in the places he goes and the friends he cultivates, what he does with his time and how he spends his money. Indeed faith leaves no area of the new believer's life unaffected.

The genuinely renewed man will have a new life center. He will experience a new orientation affecting his whole personality. He will become aware of a different philosophic outlook. Things he once held to be of value may suddenly lose all their attraction for him and he may even hate some things he formerly loved.

The man who recoils from this revolutionary kind of Christianity is retreating before the cross. But thousands do so retreat, and they try to make things right by seeking baptism and church membership. No wonder they are so dissatisfied.

On Taking Too Much for Granted

Once Mary and Joseph, with a number of friends and relatives, were traveling back home from Jerusalem and, supposing the young Jesus to be in the company, went a whole day's journey before discovering that He had been left behind.

Their fault was that they assumed that what they wanted to believe was so in fact. They took too much for granted. A simple check at the start of the journey would have saved them a harrowing experience of fear and uncertainty and two days' unnecessary travel. Theirs was a pardonable fault and one that we ourselves are in great danger of committing. The whole company of evangelicals is traveling home supposing things, some of which may not be true. We had better check before we go any further. Our failure to do so could have more serious consequences than those suffered by Mary and Joseph. It could lead straight to tragedy.

There is danger that we take Christ for granted. We "suppose" that because we hold New Testament beliefs we are therefore New Testament Christians; but it does not follow. The devil is a better theologian than any of us and is a devil still.

We may, for instance, assume that salvation is possible without repentance. Pardon without penitence is a delusion which simple honesty requires that we expose for what it is. To be forgiven, a sin must be forsaken. This accords with the Scriptures, with common logic and with the experience of the saints of all ages.

We are also in danger of assuming the value of religion without righteousness. Through the various media of public communication we are being pressured into believing that religion is little more than a beautiful thing capable of bringing courage and peace of mind to a troubled world. Let us resist this effort at brainwashing. The purpose of Christ's redeeming work was to make it possible for bad men to become good—deeply, radically and finally. God translates men out of the kingdom of darkness into the kingdom of the Son of His love. To believe that such translated men must still dwell in darkness is a reflection on the blood of Christ and the wisdom of God.

In spite of all that James said to the contrary, we are still likely to take for granted that faith without works does somehow have a mystic value after all.

But "faith . . . worketh by love" (Galatians 5:6), said Paul, and where the works of love are absent we can only conclude that faith is absent also. Faith in faith has displaced faith in God in too many places.

A whole new generation of Christians has come up believing that it is possible to "accept" Christ without forsaking the world. But what saith the Holy Ghost? "Ye adulterers and adulteresses, know ye not that the friendship of the world is enmity with God? whosoever therefore will be a friend of the world is the enemy of God" (James 4:4), and "If any man love the world, the love of the Father is not in him" (1 John 2:15). This requires no comment, only obedience.

We may also erroneously assume that we can experience justification without transformation. Justification and regeneration are not the same; they may be thought apart in theology but they can never be experienced apart in fact; when God *declares* a man righteous He instantly sets about to *make* him righteous. Our error today is that we do not expect a converted man to be a transformed man, and as a result of this error our churches are full of substandard Christians. A revival is among other things a return to the belief that real faith invariably produces holiness of heart and righteousness of life.

Again, we may go astray by assuming that we can do spiritual work without spiritual power. I have heard the notion seriously advanced that whereas once to win men to Christ it was necessary to have a gift from the Holy Spirit, now religious movies make it possible for anyone to win souls, without such spiritual anointing! "Whom the gods would destroy they first make mad." Surely such a notion is madness, but until now I have not heard it challenged among the evangelicals.

David Brainerd once compared a man without the power of the Spirit trying to do spiritual work to a workman without fingers attempting to do manual labor. The figure is striking but it does not overstate the facts. The Holy Spirit is not a luxury meant to make deluxe Christians, as an illuminated frontispiece and a leather binding make a deluxe book. The Spirit is an imperative necessity. Only the Eternal Spirit can do eternal deeds.

Without exhausting the list of things wrongly taken for granted I would mention one more: Millions take for granted that it is possible to live for Christ without first having died with Christ. This is a serious error and we dare not leave it unchallenged.

The victorious Christian has known two lives. The first was his life in Adam which was motivated by the carnal mind and can never please God in any way. It can never be converted; it can only die (Romans 8:5-8). The second life of the Christian is his new life in Christ (6:1-14). To live a Christian life with the life of Adam is wholly impossible. Yet multitudes take for granted that it can be done and go on year after year in defeat. And worst of all they accept this half-dead condition as normal.

For our own soul's sake, let's not take too much for granted.

The Cure for a Fretful Spirit

The Holy Spirit in Psalm 37:1 admonishes us to beware of irritation in our religious lives: *"Fret not thyself because of evildoers, neither be thou envious against the workers of iniquity."*

The word "fret" comes to us from the Anglo-Saxon and carries with it such a variety of meanings as bring a rather pained smile to our faces. Notice how they expose us and locate us behind our disguises. The primary meaning of the word is to eat, and from there it has been extended with rare honesty to cover most of the manifestations of an irritable disposition. "To eat away; to gnaw; to chafe; to gall; to vex; to worry; to agitate; to wear away"; so says Webster, and all who have felt the exhausting, corrosive effects of fretfulness know how accurately the description fits the facts.

Now, the grace of God in the human heart works to calm the agitation that normally accompanies life in such a world as ours. The Holy Spirit acts as a lubricant to reduce the friction to a minimum and to stop the fretting and chafing in their grosser phases. But for most of us the problem is not as simple as that.

Fretfulness may be trimmed down to the ground and its roots remain alive deep within the soul, there growing and extending themselves all unsuspected, sending up their old poisonous shoots under other names and other appearances.

It was not to the unregenerate that the words "Fret not" were spoken, but to God-fearing persons capable of understanding spiritual things. We Christians need to watch and pray lest we fall into this temptation and spoil our Christian testimony by an irritable spirit under the stress and strain of life.

It requires great care and a true knowledge of ourselves to distinguish a spiritual burden from religious irritation. We cannot close our minds to everything that is happening around us. We dare not rest at ease in Zion when the Church is so desperately in need of spiritually sensitive men and women who can see her faults and try to call her back to the path of righteousness. The prophets and apostles of Bible times carried in their hearts such crushing burdens for God's wayward people that they could say, "Tears have been my meat day and night" (Psalm 42:3), and "Oh that my head were waters, and mine eyes a fountain of tears, that I might weep day and night for the slain of the daughter of my people!" (Jeremiah 9:1). These men were heavy with a true burden. What they felt was not vexation but acute concern for the honor of God and the souls of men.

By nature some persons fret easily. They have difficulty separating their personal antipathies from the burden of the Spirit. When they are grieved they can hardly say whether it is a pure and charitable thing or merely irritation set up by other Christians having opinions different from their own.

Of one thing we may be sure: we can never escape the external stimuli that cause vexation. The world is full of them, and though we were to retreat to a cave and live the remainder of our days alone we still could not lose them. The rough floor of our cave would chafe us, the weather would irritate us and the very silence would cause us to fret.

Deliverance from a fretting spirit may be by blood and fire, by humility, self-abnegation and a patient carrying of the cross. There will always be "evildoers" and "workers of iniquity," and for the most part they will appear to succeed while the forces of righteousness will seem to fail. The wicked will always have the money and the talent and the publicity and the numbers, while the righteous will be few and poor and unknown. The prayerless Christian will surely misread the signs and fret against the circumstances. That is what the Spirit warns us against.

Let us look out calmly upon the world; or better yet, let us look down upon it from above where Christ is seated and we are seated in Him. Though the wicked spread himself like "a green bay tree," it is only for a moment. Soon he passes away and is not. "But the salvation of the righteous is of the LORD: he is their strength in the time of trouble" (Psalm 37:39). This knowledge should cure the fretting spirit.

CHAPTER

18

Boasting or Belittling

We all know how painful it is to be forced to listen to a confirmed boaster sound off on his favorite topic—himself. To be the captive of such a man even for a short time tries our patience to the utmost and puts a heavy strain upon our Christian charity.

Boasting is particularly offensive when it is heard among the children of God, the one place above all others where it should never be found. Yet it is quite common among Christians, though disguised somewhat by the use of the stock expression, "I say this to the glory of God."

Some boasters appear to feel a bit self-conscious, and apologize meekly for their outbursts of self-praise. Others have accepted themselves as being all their doting relatives and friends claim they are and habitually speak of themselves in reverent terms, as if their superiority was a matter of common knowledge too well established to require proof. Such a one was the concert singer who replied to a glowing compliment after a performance, "Well, what did you expect?"

God is very patient with His children and often tolerates in them carnal traits so gross as to shock their fellow Christians. But that is only for a while. As more light comes to our hearts, and especially as we go on to new and advanced spiritual experiences, God begins to impose disciplines upon us to purge us from the same faults He tolerated before. Then He permits us to say and do things that react unfavorably against us and expose our vanity for what it is. It may then happen in the providential will of God that the very gift we have boasted of may be lost to us or the project we are so proud of will fail. After we have learned our lesson the Lord may restore what He has taken away, for He is more concerned with our souls than with our service. But sometimes our boasting permanently hurts us and excludes us from blessings we might have enjoyed.

Another habit not quite so odious is belittling ourselves. This might seem to be the exact opposite of boasting, but actually it is the same old sin traveling under a *nom de plume*. It is simply egoism trying to act spiritual. It is impatient Saul hastily offering an unacceptable sacrifice to the Lord.

Self-derogation is bad for the reason that self must be there to derogate. Self, whether swaggering or groveling, can never be anything but hateful to God.

Boasting is an evidence that we are pleased with self; belittling, that we are disappointed in it. Either way we reveal that we have a high opinion of ourselves. The belittler is chagrined that one as obviously superior as he should not have done better, and he punishes himself by making uncomplimentary remarks about himself. That he does not really mean what he says may be proved quite easily. Let someone else say the same things. His eager defense of himself will reveal how he feels and has secretly felt all the time.

The victorious Christian neither exalts nor downgrades himself. His interests have shifted from self to Christ. What he is or is not no longer concerns him. He believes that he has been crucified with Christ and he is not willing either to praise or deprecate such a man.

Yet the knowledge that he has been crucified is only half the victory. "Nevertheless I live; yet not I, but Christ liveth in me: and the life which I now live in the flesh I live by the faith of the Son of God, who loved me, and gave himself for me" (Galatians 2:20). Christ is now where the man's ego was formerly. The man is now Christ-centered instead of self-centered, and he forgets himself in his delighted preoccupation with Christ.

Candor compels me to acknowledge that it is a lot easier to write about this than it is to live it. Self is one of the toughest plants that grows in the garden of life. It is, in fact, indestructible by any human means. Just when we are sure it is dead it turns up somewhere as robust as ever to trouble our peace and poison the fruit of our lives.

Yet there is deliverance. When our judicial crucifixion becomes actual the victory is near; and when our faith rises to claim the risen life of Christ as our own the triumph is complete. The trouble is that we do not receive the benefits of all this until something radical has happened in our own experience, something which in its psychological effects approaches actual crucifixion. What Christ went through we also must go through. Rejection, surrender, loss, a violent detachment from the world, the pain of social ostracism—all must be felt in our actual experience.

Where we have failed is in the practical application of the teaching concerning the crucified life. Too many have been content to be armchair Christians, satisfied with the theology of the cross. Plainly Christ never intended that we should rest in a mere theory of self-denial. His teaching identified His disciples with Himself so intimately that they would have had to be extremely dull not to have understood that they were expected to experience very much the same pain and loss as He Himself did.

The healthy soul is the victorious soul and victory never comes while self is permitted to remain unjudged and uncrucified. While we boast or belittle we may be perfectly sure that the cross has not yet done its work within us. Faith and obedience will bring the cross into the life and cure both habits.

The Communion of Saints

"I believe in the communion of saints."
—Apostles' Creed

T hese words were written into the creed about the middle of the fifth century.

It would be difficult if not altogether impossible for us at this late date to know exactly what was in the minds of the Church fathers who introduced the words into the creed, but in the book of Acts we have a description of the first Christian communion: "Then they that gladly received his word were baptized; and the same day there were added unto them about three thousand souls. And they continued stedfastly in the apostles' doctrine and fellowship, and in breaking of bread, and in prayers" (2:41-42).

Here is the original apostolic fellowship, the pattern after which every true Christian communion must be modeled.

The word "fellowship," in spite of its abuses, is still a beautiful and meaningful word. When rightly understood it means the same as the word "communion," that is, the act and condition of sharing together in some common blessing by numbers of persons. The communion of saints, then, means an intimate and loving sharing together of certain spiritual blessings by persons who are on an equal footing before the blessing in which they share. This fellowship must include every member of the Church of God from Pentecost to this present moment and on to the end of the age.

Now, before there can be *communion* there must be *union*. The sharers are one in a sense altogether above organization, nationality, race or denomination. That oneness is a divine thing, achieved by the Holy Spirit in the act of regeneration. Whoever is born of God is one with everyone else who is born of God. Just as gold is always gold, wherever and in whatever shape it is found, and every detached scrap of gold belongs to the true family and is composed of the same element, so every regenerate soul belongs to the universal Christian community and to the fellowship of the saints.

Every redeemed soul is born out of the same spiritual life as every other redeemed soul and partakes of the divine nature in exactly the same manner. Each one is thus made a member of the Christian community and a sharer in everything which that community enjoys. This is the true communion of saints. But to know this is not enough. If we would enter into the power of it we must exercise ourselves in this truth; we must *practice* thinking and praying with the thought that we are members of the Body of Christ and brothers to all the ransomed saints living and dead who have believed on Christ and acknowledged Him as Lord.

We have said that the communion of saints is a fellowship, a sharing in certain divinely given things by divinely called persons. Now, what are those things?

The first and most important is *life*—"the life of God in the soul of man," to borrow a phrase from Henry Scougal. This life is the basis of everything else which is given and shared. And that life is nothing else than God Himself. It should be evident that there can be no true Christian sharing unless there is first an impartation of life. An organization and a name do not make a church. One hundred religious persons knit into a unity by careful organization do not constitute a church any more than eleven dead men make a football team. The first requisite is life, always.

The apostolic fellowship is also a fellowship of *truth*. The inclusiveness of the fellowship must always be held along with the exclusiveness of it. Truth brings into its gracious circle all who admit and accept the Bible as the source of all truth and the Son of God as the Savior of men. But there dare be no weak compromise with the facts, no sentimental mouthing of the old phrases: "We are all headed for the same place. . . . Each one is seeking in his own way to please the Father and make heaven his home." The truth makes men free, and the truth will bind and loose, will open and shut, will include and exclude at its high will without respect to persons. To reject or deny the truth of the Word is to exclude ourselves from the apostolic communion.

Now, someone may ask, "What is the truth of which you speak? Is my fate to depend upon Baptist truth or Presbyterian truth or Anglican truth, or all of these or none of these? To know the communion of saints must I believe in Calvinism or Arminianism? In the Congregational or the Episcopal form of church government? Must I interpret prophecy in accord with the premillenarians or the postmillenarians? Must I believe in immersion or sprinkling or pouring?" The answer to all this is easy. The confusion is only apparent, not actual.

The early Christians, under the fire of persecution, driven from place to place, sometimes deprived of the opportunity for careful instruction in the faith, wanted a "rule" which would sum up all that they must believe to assure their everlasting welfare. Out of this critical need arose the creeds. Of the many, the Apostles' Creed is the best known and best loved, and has been reverently repeated by the largest number of believers through the centuries. And for millions of good men that creed contains the essentials of truth. Not all truths, to be sure, but the heart of all truth. It served in trying days as a kind of secret password that instantly united men to each other when passed from lip to lip by the followers of the Lamb. It is fair to say, then, that the truth shared by saints in the apostolic fellowship is the same truth which is outlined for convenience in the Apostles' Creed.

In this day when the truth of Christianity is under serious fire from so many directions it is most important that we know what we believe and that we guard it carefully. But in our effort to interpret and expound the Holy Scriptures in accord with the ancient faith of all Christians, we should remember that a seeking soul may find salvation through the blood of Christ while yet knowing little of the fuller teachings of Christian theology. We must, therefore, admit to our fellowship every sheep who has heard the voice of the Shepherd and has tried to follow Him.

The beginner in Christ who has not yet had time to learn much Christian truth and the underprivileged believer who has had the misfortune to be brought up in a church where the Word has been neglected from the pulpit are very much in the same situation. Their faith grasps only a small portion of truth, and their "sharing" is necessarily limited to the small portion they grasp. The important thing, however, is that the little bit they do enjoy is *real truth*. It may be no more than this, that "Christ Jesus came into the world to save sinners"; but if they walk in the light of that much truth, no more is required to bring them into the circle of the blessed and to constitute them true members of the apostolic fellowship.

Then, true Christian communion consists in the sharing of a *Presence*. This is not poetry merely, but a fact taught in bold letters in the New Testament.

God has given us Himself in the Person of His Son. "Where two or three are gathered together in my name, there am I in the midst of them" (Matthew 18:20). The immanence of God in His universe makes possible the enjoyment of the "real Presence" by the saints of God in heaven and on earth simultaneously. Wherever they may be, He is present to them in the fullness of His Godhead.

I do not believe that the Bible teaches the possibility of communication between the saints on earth and those in heaven. But while there cannot be communication, there most surely can be communion. Death does not tear the individual believer from his place in the Body of Christ. As in our human bodies each member is nourished by the same blood which at once gives life and unity to the entire organism, so in the Body of Christ the quickening Spirit flowing through every part gives life and unity to the whole. Our Christian brethren who have gone from our sight retain still their place in the universal fellowship. The Church is one, whether waking or sleeping, by a unity of life forevermore.

The most important thing about the doctrine of the communion of saints is its practical effects on the lives of Christians. We know very little about the saints above, but about the saints on earth we know, or can know, a great deal. We Protestants do not believe (since the Bible does not teach) that the saints who have gone into heaven before us are in any way affected by the prayers or labors of saints who remain on earth. Our particular care is not for those whom God has already honored with the vision beatific, but for the hard-pressed and struggling pilgrims who are still traveling toward the City of God. We all belong to each other; the spiritual welfare of each one is or should be the loving concern of all the rest.

We should pray for an enlargement of soul to receive into our hearts all of God's people, whatever their race, color or church affiliation. Then we should practice thinking of ourselves as members of the blessed family of God and should strive in prayer to love and appreciate everyone who is born of the Father.

I suggest also that we try to acquaint ourselves as far as possible with the good and saintly souls who lived before our times and now belong to the company of the redeemed in heaven. How sad to limit our sympathies to those of our own day, when God in His providence has made it possible for us to enjoy the rich treasures of the minds and hearts of so many holy and gifted saints of other days. To confine our reading to the works of a few favorite authors of today or last week is to restrict our horizons and to pinch our souls dangerously.

I have no doubt that the prayerful reading of some of the great spiritual classics of the centuries would destroy in us forever that constriction of soul which seems to be the earmark of modern evangelicalism.

For many of us the wells of the past wait to be reopened. Augustine, for instance, would bring to us a sense of the overwhelming majesty of God that would go far to cure the flippancy of spirit found so widely among modern Christians. Bernard of Cluny would sing to us of "Jerusalem the Golden" and the peace of an eternal sabbath day until the miserable pleasures of this world become intolerable; Richard Rolle would show us how to escape from "the abundance of riches, the flattering of women and the fairness of youth," that we may go on to know God with an intimacy that will become in our hearts "heat, fragrance and song"; Tersteegen would whisper to us of the "hidden love of God" and the awful Presence until our hearts would become "still before Him" and "prostrate inwardly adore Him"; before our eyes the sweet St. Francis would throw his arms of love around sun and moon, trees and rain, bird and beast, and thank God for them all in a pure rapture of spiritual devotion.

But who is able to complete the roster of the saints? To them we owe a debt of gratitude too great to comprehend: prophet and apostle, martyr and reformer, scholar and translator, hymnist and composer, teacher and evangelist, not to mention ten thousand times ten thousand simplehearted and anonymous souls who kept the flame of pure religion alive even in those times when the faith of our fathers was burning but dimly all over the world.

They belong to us, all of them, and we belong to them. They and we and all redeemed men and women of whatever age or clime are included in the universal fellowship of Christ, and together compose "a royal priesthood, an holy nation, a peculiar people" (1 Peter 2:9), who enjoy a common but blessed communion of saints.

From *Foundations of the Faith*, Fleming H. Revell, Westwood, N.J. Used by permission.

Temperament in the Christian Life

A celebrated American preacher once advanced the novel theory that the various denominations with their different doctrinal emphases served a useful purpose as gathering places for persons of similar temperaments. Christians, he suggested, tend to gravitate toward others of like mental types. Hence the denominations.

Undoubtedly this is oversimplification carried to the point of error. There are too many persons of dissimilar temperaments in every denomination to support such a sweeping classification. Yet I believe that we have here an instance where an error may serve to point up a truth, the truth being that temperament has a great deal to do with our religious views and with the emphases we lay on spiritual matters generally.

It may be a bit difficult to determine which is cause and which effect, but I have noticed that historically Calvinism has flourished among peoples of a markedly phlegmatic disposition. While it is true that Jacob Arminius was a Dutchman, on the whole the Dutch people appear temperamentally quite suited to Calvinism. On the other hand, it would be hard to imagine a Calvinistic Spaniard or Italian. Isolated instances there certainly are, but for the most part the buoyant, volatile, mandolin-playing Latin does not take naturally to long periods of meditation on the divine sovereignty and the eternal decrees.

While we all pride ourselves that we draw our beliefs from the Holy Scriptures, along those borderlines where good men disagree we may unconsciously take sides with our temperament. Cast of mind may easily determine our views when the Scriptures are not clear. People may be classified roughly into two psychological types, the lighthearted and the somber, and it is easy to see how each type will be attracted to the doctrinal views that agree most naturally with its own mental cast. The Calvinist, for instance, never permits himself to become too happy, while the Arminian tends to equate gravity of disposition with coldness of heart and tries to cure it with a revival.

No Calvinist could have written the radiant hymns of Bernard of Clairvaux or Charles Wesley. Calvinism never produced a Christian mystic, unless we except John Newton who was near to being a mystic and did write a few hymns almost

as radiant as those of Bernard. To square the re-
cords, however, it should be said that if the Calvinist does not rise as high he usually stays up
longer. He places more emphasis on the Holy
Scriptures which never change, while his opposite number (as the newspapers say) tends to
judge his spiritual condition by the state of his
feelings, which change constantly. This may be
the reason that so many Calvinistic churches remain orthodox for centuries, at least in doctrine,
while many churches of the Arminian persuasion
often go liberal in one generation.

I realize that I am doing a bit of oversimplifying
on my own here; still I believe there is more than a
germ of truth in the whole thing. Anyway, I am
less concerned with the effect of temperament on
the historic Church, which obviously I can do
nothing about, than with its effect upon my own
soul and the souls of my readers, whom I may be
able to influence somewhat.

Whether or not my broader conclusions are
sound, there would seem to be no reason to doubt
that we naturally tend to interpret Scripture in
the light (or shadow) of our own temperament
and let our peculiar mental cast decide the degree
of importance we attach to various religious doctrines and practices.

The odd thing about this human quirk is that it
prospers most where there is the greatest amount
of religious freedom. The authoritarian churches
that tell their adherents exactly what to believe
and where to lay their emphasis produce a fair

degree of uniformity among their members. By stretching everyone on the bed of Procrustes they manage to lengthen or trim back the individual temperament to their liking. The free Protestant, who is still permitted a certain amount of private interpretation, is much more likely to fall into the trap of temperament. Exposure to this temptation is one price he pays for his freedom.

The minister above all others should look deep into his own heart to discover the reason for his more pronounced views. It is not enough to draw himself up and declare with dignity that he preaches the Bible and nothing but the Bible. That claim is made by every man who stands in sincerity to declare the truth; but truth has many facets, and the man of God is in grave danger of revealing only a limited few to his people, and those the ones he by disposition favors most.

One cannot imagine Francis of Assisi preaching Edwards' sermon, "Sinners in the Hands of an Angry God," nor can we picture Jonathan Edwards preaching to the birds or calling upon sun and moon and wind and stars to join him in praising the Lord. Yet both were good men who loved God deeply and trusted Christ completely. Many other factors besides temperament must not be overlooked.

Are we then to accept the bias of disposition as something inevitable? Are we to allow our religious views to be dictated by ancestors long dead whose genes still stir within us? By no means. The Scriptures, critical self-discipline, honesty of heart and increased trust in the inward operations of the Holy Spirit will save us from being too greatly influenced by temperament.

Does God Always Answer Prayer?

Contrary to popular opinion, the cultivation of a psychology of uncritical belief is not an unqualified good, and if carried too far it may be a positive evil. The whole world has been booby-trapped by the devil, and the deadliest trap of all is the religious one. Error never looks so innocent as when it is found in the sanctuary.

One field where harmless-looking but deadly traps appear in great profusion is the field of prayer. There are more sweet notions about prayer than could be contained in a large book, all of them wrong and all highly injurious to the souls of men.

I think of one such false notion that is found often in pleasant places consorting smilingly with other notions of unquestionable orthodoxy. It is that *God always answers prayer*.

This error appears among the saints as a kind of all-purpose philosophic therapy to prevent any disappointed Christian from suffering too great a shock when it becomes evident to him that his prayer expectations are not being fulfilled. It is explained that God always answers prayer, either by saying Yes or by saying No, or by substituting something else for the desired favor.

Now, it would be hard to invent a neater trick than this to save face for the petitioner whose requests have been rejected for nonobedience. Thus when a prayer is not answered he has but to smile brightly and explain, "God said No." It is all so very comfortable. His wobbly faith is saved from confusion and his conscience is permitted to lie undisturbed. But I wonder if it is honest.

To receive an answer to prayer as the Bible uses the term and as Christians have understood it historically, two elements must be present: (1) A clear-cut request made to God for a specific favor. (2) A clear-cut granting of that favor by God in answer to the request. There must be no semantic twisting, no changing of labels, no altering of the map during the journey to help the embarrassed tourist to find himself.

When we go to God with a request that He modify the existing situation for us, that is, that He answer prayer, there are two conditions that we must meet: (1) We must pray in the will of God and (2) we must be on what old-fashioned Christians often call "praying ground"; that is, we must be living lives pleasing to God.

It is futile to beg God to act contrary to His revealed purposes. To pray with confidence the petitioner must be certain that his request falls within the broad will of God for His people.

The second condition is also vitally important. God has not placed Himself under obligation to honor the requests of worldly, carnal or disobedient Christians. He hears and answers the prayers only of those who walk in His way.

> Beloved, if our heart condemn us not, then have we confidence toward God. And whatsoever we ask, we receive of him, because we keep his commandments, and do those things that are pleasing in his sight. . . . If ye abide in me, and my words abide in you, ye shall ask what ye will, and it shall be done unto you. (1 John 3:21-22; John 15:7)

God wants us to pray and He wants to answer our prayers, but He makes our use of prayer as a privilege to commingle with His use of prayer as a discipline. To receive answers to prayer we must meet God's terms. If we neglect His commandments our petitions will not be honored. He will alter situations only at the request of obedient and humble souls.

The God-always-answers-prayer sophistry leaves the praying man without discipline. By the exercise of this bit of smooth casuistry he ignores the necessity to live soberly, righteously and godly in this present world, and actually takes God's flat refusal to answer his prayer as the very answer itself. Of course such a man will not grow in holiness; he will never learn how to wrestle and wait; he will never know correction; he will not hear the voice of God calling him forward; he will never arrive at the place where he is morally and spiritually fit to have his prayers answered. His wrong philosophy has ruined him.

That is why I turn aside to expose the bit of bad theology upon which his bad philosophy is founded. The man who accepts it never knows where he stands; he never knows whether or not he has true faith, for if his request is not granted he avoids the implication by the simple dodge of declaring that God switched the whole thing around and gave him something else. He will not allow himself to shoot at a target, so he cannot tell how good or how bad a marksman he is.

Of certain persons James says plainly: "Ye ask, and receive not, because ye ask amiss, that ye may consume it upon your lusts" (4:3). From that brief sentence we may learn that God refuses some requests because they who make them are not morally worthy to receive the answer. But this means nothing to the one who has been seduced into the belief that God always answers prayer. When such a man asks and receives not he passes his hand over the hat and comes up with the answer in some other form. One thing he clings to with great tenacity: God never turns anyone away, but invariably grants every request.

The truth is that God always answers the prayer that accords with His will as revealed in the Scriptures, provided the one who prays is obedient and trustful. Further than this we dare not go.

Self-deception and How to Avoid It

Of all forms of deception self-deception is the most deadly, and of all deceived persons the self-deceived are the least likely to discover the fraud.

The reason for this is simple. When a man is deceived by another he is deceived against his will. He is contending against an adversary and is temporarily the victim of the other's guile. Since he expects his foe to take advantage of him he is watchful and quick to suspect trickery. Under such circumstances it is possible to be deceived sometimes and for a short while, but because the victim is resisting he may break out of the trap and escape before too long. With the self-deceived it is quite different. He is his own enemy and is working a fraud upon himself.

He wants to believe the lie and is psychologically conditioned to do so. He does not resist the deceit but collaborates with it against himself. There is no struggle, because the victim surrenders before the fight begins. He enjoys being deceived.

It is altogether possible to practice fraud upon our own souls and go deceived to judgment. "If a man think himself to be something, when he is nothing," said Paul, "he deceiveth himself" (Galatians 6:3). With this agrees the inspired James: "If any man among you seem to be religious, and bridleth not his tongue, but deceiveth his own heart, this man's religion is vain" (James 1:26).

The farther we push into the sanctuary the greater becomes the danger of self-deception. The deeply religious man is far more vulnerable than the easygoing fellow who takes his religion lightly. This latter may be deceived but he is not likely to be self-deceived.

Under the pressure of deep spiritual concern, and before his heart has been wholly conquered by the Spirit of God, a man may be driven to try every dodge to save face and preserve a semblance of his old independence. This is always dangerous and if persisted in may prove calamitous.

The fallen heart is by nature idolatrous. There appears to be no limit to which some of us will go to save our idol, while at the same time telling ourselves eagerly that we are trusting in Christ alone. It takes a violent act of renunciation to deliver us from the hidden idol; and since very few modern Christians understand that such an act is necessary, and only a small number of those who know are willing to do, it follows that relatively few professors of the Christian faith these days have ever experienced the painful act of renunciation that frees the heart from idolatry.

Prayer is usually recommended as the panacea for all ills and the key to open every prison door, and it would indeed be difficult to overstate the advantages and privilege of Spirit-inspired prayer. But we must not forget that unless we are wise and watchful prayer itself may become a source of self-deception. There are as many kinds of prayer as there are problems and some kinds are not acceptable to God. The prophets of the Old Testament denounced Israel for trying to hide their iniquities behind their prayers. Christ flatly rejected the prayers of hypocrites and James declared that some religious persons ask and receive not because they ask amiss.

To escape self-deception the praying man must come out clean and honest. He cannot hide in the cross while concealing in his bosom the golden wedge and the goodly Babylonish garment. Grace will save a man but it will not save him and his idol. The blood of Christ will shield the penitent sinner alone, but never the sinner and his idol. Faith will justify the sinner, but it will never justify the sinner and his sin.

No amount of pleading will make evil good or wrong right. A man may engage in a great deal of humble talk before God and get no response because unknown to himself he is using prayer to disguise disobedience. He may lie for hours in sackcloth and ashes with no higher motive than to try to persuade God to come over on his side so he can have his own way. He may grovel before God in a welter of self-accusation, refuse to give up his secret sin and be rejected for his pains. It can happen.

Dr. H.M. Shuman once said to me in private conversation that he believed the one quality God required a man to have before He would save him was honesty. With this I heartily agree. However dishonest the man may have been before, he must put away his duplicity if he is to be accepted before the Lord. Double-dealing is unutterably offensive to God. The insincere man has no claim on mercy. For such a man the cross of Christ provides no remedy. Christ can and will save a man who *has been* dishonest, but He cannot save him *while* he is dishonest. Absolute candor is an indispensable requisite to salvation.

How may we remain free from self-deception? The answer sounds old-fashioned and dull but here it is: Mean what you say and never say what you do not mean, either to God or man. Think candid thoughts and act forthrightly always, whatever the consequence. To do this will bring the cross into your life and keep you dead to self and to public opinion. And it may get you into trouble sometimes, too. But a guileless mind is a great treasure; it is worth any price.

On Breeding Spotted Mice

The Associated Press lately carried an interesting if somewhat depressing story out of London about a certain British peer who had died just a few days short of his eighty-ninth birthday.

Having been a man of means and position, it had presumably not been necessary for him to work for a living like the rest of us, so at the time of his death he had had about seventy adult years in which he was free to do whatever he wanted to do, to pursue any calling he wished or to work at anything he felt worthy of his considerable abilities.

And what had he chosen to do? Well, according to the story, he had "devoted his life to trying to breed the perfect spotted mouse."

Now, I grant every man the right to breed spotted mice if he wants to and can get the cooperation of the mice, and I freely admit that it is his business and not mine. Not being a mouse lover (nor a mouse hater for that matter; I am just neutral about mice), I do not know but that a spotted mouse might be more useful and make a more affectionate pet than a common mouse-colored mouse. But still I am troubled.

The mouse breeder in question was a lord, and I was born on a farm in the hill country of Pennsylvania, but since a cat can look at a king I suppose a farm boy can look at a lord, even look at him with disapproval if the circumstances warrant. Anyway, a man's a man for a' that, and I feel a certain kinship for every man born of woman; so I cannot but grieve for my brother beyond the seas.

Made in the image of God, equipped with awesome powers of mind and soul, called to dream immortal dreams and to think the long thoughts of eternity, he chooses the breeding of a spotted mouse as his reason for existing. Invited to walk with God on earth and to dwell at last with the saints and angels in the world above; called to serve his generation by the will of God, to press with holy vigor toward the mark for the prize of the high calling of God in Christ Jesus, he dedicates his life to the spotted mouse—not just evenings or holidays, mind you, but his entire life. Surely this is tragedy worthy of the mind of an Aeschylus or a Shakespeare.

Let us hope that the story is not true or that the newsboys got it mixed up as they sometimes do; but even if the whole thing should prove to be a hoax, still it points up a stark human tragedy that is being enacted before our eyes daily, not by make-believe play actors, but by real men and women who are the characters they portray. These should be concerned with sin and righteousness and judgment; they should be getting ready to die and to live again; but instead they spend their days breeding spotted mice.

If the spiritual view of the world is the correct one, as Christianity boldly asserts that it is, then for every one of us heaven is more important than earth and eternity more important than time. If Jesus Christ is who He claimed to be; if He is what the glorious company of the apostles and the noble army of martyrs declared that He is; if the faith which the holy Church throughout all the world doth acknowledge is the true faith of God, then no man has any right to dedicate his life to anything that can burn or rust or rot or die. No man has any right to give himself completely to anyone but Christ nor to anything but prayer.

The man who does not know where he is is lost; the man who does not know why he was born is worse lost; the man who cannot find an object worthy of his true devotion is lost utterly; and by this description the human race is lost and it is a part of our lostness that we do not know how lost we are. So we use up the few precious years allotted to us breeding spotted mice. Not the kind that scurry and squeak, maybe; but viewed in the light of eternity, are not most of our little human activities almost as meaningless?

One of the glories of the Christian gospel is its ability not only to deliver a man from sin but to orient him, to place him on a peak from which he can see yesterday and today in their relation to tomorrow. The truth cleanses his mind so that he can recognize things that matter and see time and space and kings and cabbages in their true perspective. The Spirit-illuminated Christian cannot be cheated, He knows the values of things; he will not bid on a rainbow nor make a down payment on a mirage; he will not, in short, devote his life to spotted mice.

Back of every wasted life is a bad philosophy, an erroneous conception of life's worth and purpose. The man who believes that he was born to get all he can will spend his life trying to get it; and whatever he gets will be but a cage of spotted mice. The man who believes he was created to enjoy fleshly pleasures will devote himself to pleasure seeking; and if by a combination of favorable circumstances he manages to get a lot of fun out of life, his pleasures will all turn to ashes in his mouth at the last. He will find out too late that God made him too noble to be satisfied with those tawdry pleasures he had devoted his life to here under the sun.

The Unknown Saints

William Wordsworth, in a fine passage, states his belief that there are many more poets in the world than we suppose,

> ... *men endowed with highest gifts,*
> *The vision and the faculty divine,*

but who are unknown because they lacked or failed to cultivate the gift of versification.

Then he sums up his belief in a sentence that suggests truth far beyond any that he had in mind at the time:

> *Strongest minds*
> *Are often those of whom the noisy world*
> *Hears least.*

Most of us in our soberer moments would admit the soundness of this observation, but the hard fact is that for the average person it is not the findings of the sober moment that determine our total working philosophy; rather it is the shallow and deceptive notions pressed upon us by the "noisy world." Human society generally (and especially in the United States) has fallen into the error of assuming that greatness and fame are synonymous. Americans appear to take for granted that each generation provides a certain number of superior men and the democratic processes unerringly find those men and set them in a place of prominence. How wrong can people get!

We have but to become acquainted with, or even listen to, the big names of our times to discover how wretchedly inferior most of them are. Many appear to have arrived at their present eminence by pull, brass, nerve, gall and lucky accident. We turn away from them sick to our stomach and wonder for a discouraged moment if this is the best the human race can produce. But we gain our self-possession again by the simple expedient of recalling some of the plain men we know, who live unheralded and unsung, and who are made of stuff infinitely finer than the hoarse-voiced braggarts who occupy too many of the highest offices in the land.

If we would see life steadily and see it whole we must make a stern effort to break away from the power of that false philosophy that equates greatness with fame. The two may be and often are oceans and continents apart.

If the Church were a body wholly unaffected by the world we could toss the above problem over to the secular philosophers and go about our business; but the truth is that the Church also suffers from this evil notion. Christians have fallen into the habit of accepting the noisiest and most notorious among them as the best and the greatest. They too have learned to equate popularity with excellence, and in open defiance of the Sermon on the Mount they have given their approval not to the meek but to the self-assertive; not to the mourner but to the self-assured; not to the pure in heart who see God but to the publicity hunter who seeks headlines.

If we might paraphrase Wordsworth we could make his lines run,

> *Purest saints*
> *Are often these of whom the noisy church*
> *Hears least,*

and the words would be true, deeply, wonderfully true.

After more than thirty years of observing the religious scene I have been forced to conclude that saintliness and church leadership are not often synonymous. I have on many occasions preached to grateful Christians who had gone so much farther than I had into the sweet mysteries of God that I actually felt unworthy to tie their shoelaces. Yet they sat meekly listening while one inferior to them stood in the place of prominence and declared imperfectly truths with which they had long been familiar by intimate and beautiful experience. They must have known and felt how much of theory and how little of real heart knowledge there was in the sermon, but they said nothing and no doubt appreciated what little of good there was in the message.

Were the Church a pure and Spirit-filled body, wholly led and directed by spiritual considerations, certainly the purest and the saintliest men and women would be the ones most appreciated and most honored; but the opposite is true. Godliness is no longer valued, except for the very old or the very dead. The saintly souls are forgotten in the whirl of religious activity. The noisy, the self-assertive, the entertaining are sought after and rewarded in every way, with gifts, crowds, offerings and publicity. The Christlike, the self-forgetting, the other-worldly are jostled aside to make room for the latest converted playboy who is usually not too well converted and still very much of a playboy.

The whole shortsighted philosophy that ignores eternal qualities and majors on trivialities is a form of unbelief. These Christians who embody such a philosophy are clamoring after present reward; they are too impatient to await the Lord's time. They will not abide the day when Christ shall make known the secret of every man's heart and reward each one according to his deeds. The true saint sees farther than this; he cares little for passing values; he looks forward eagerly to the day when eternal things shall come into their own and godliness will be found to be all that matters.

Strange as it may be, the holiest souls who have ever lived have earned the reputation for being pessimistic. Their smiling indifference to the world's attractions and their steady resistance to its temptations have been misunderstood by shallow thinkers and attributed to an unsocial spirit and a lack of love for mankind. What the world failed to see was that these peculiar men and women were beholding a city invisible; they were walking day by day in the light of another and eternal kingdom. They were already tasting the powers of the world to come and enjoying afar the triumph of Christ and the glories of the new creation.

No, the unknown saints are not pessimists, nor are they misanthropes or joy-killers. They are by virtue of their godly faith the world's only true optimists. Their creed was stated simply by Julian of Norwich when she said, "But all shall be well, and all shall be well, and all manner of thing shall be well." Though sin is in the world, she argued, a frightful visitation to be reckoned with, yet so perfect is the atonement that the time will come when all evil shall be eradicated and everything restored again to its pristine beauty in Christ. Then "all shall be well, and all manner of thing shall be well."

The wise Christian will be content to wait for that day. In the meantime, he will serve his generation in the will of God. If he should be overlooked in the religious popularity contests he will give it but small attention. He knows whom he is trying to please and he is willing to let the world think what it will of him. He will not be around much longer anyway, and where he is going men will be known not by their Hooper rating—a popularity rating of radio performers—but by the holiness of their character.

Three Faithful Wounds

"Faithful are the wounds of a friend," says the Holy Spirit in Proverbs 27:6. And lest we imagine that the preacher is the one who does the wounding, I want to quote Job 5:17 and 18: "Behold, happy is the man whom God correcteth: therefore despise not thou the chastening of the Almighty: for he maketh sore, and bindeth up: he woundeth, and his hands make whole." You see, the one who does the wounding here is not the servant, but the Master Himself. So with that in our minds I want to talk to you about three faithful wounds of a friend.

In order to get launched into my message let me introduce a little lady who has been dead for about six hundred years. She once lived and loved and prayed and sang in the city of Norwich, England. This little woman hadn't much light and she hadn't any way to get much light, but the beautiful thing about her was that, with what little biblical light she had, she walked with God so wonderfully close that she became as fragrant as a flower. And long before Reformation times she was in spirit an evangelical. She lived and died and has now been with her Lord nearly six hundred years, but she has left behind her a fragrance of Christ.

England was a better place because this little lady lived. She wrote only one book, a very tiny book that you could slip into your side pocket or your purse, but it's so flavorful, so divine, so heavenly that it has made a distinct contribution to the great spiritual literature of the world. The lady to whom I refer is the one called the Lady Julian.

Before she blossomed out into this radiant, glorious life which made her famous as a great Christian all over her part of the world, she prayed a prayer and God answered. It is this prayer with which I am concerned tonight. The essence of her prayer was this:

"O God, please give me three wounds; the wound of *contrition* and the wound of *compassion* and the wound of *longing after God.*" Then she added this little postscript which I think is one of the most beautiful things I have ever read: "This I ask without condition." She wasn't dickering with God. She wanted three things and they were all for God's glory: "I ask this without condition, Father; do what I ask and then send me the bill. Anything that it costs will be all right with me."

All great Christians have been wounded souls. It is strange what a wound will do to a man. Here's a soldier who goes out to the battlefield. He is full of jokes and strength and self-assurance; then one day a piece of shrapnel tears through him and he falls, a whimpering, beaten, defeated man. Suddenly his whole world collapses around him and this man, instead of being the great, strong, broad-chested fellow that he thought he was, suddenly becomes a whimpering boy again. And such have ever been known, I am told, to cry for their mothers when they lie bleeding and suffering on the field of battle. There is nothing like a wound to take the self-assurance out of us, to reduce us to childhood again and make us small and helpless in our own sight.

Many of the Old Testament characters were wounded men, stricken of God and afflicted indeed as their Lord was after them. Take Jacob, for instance. Twice God afflicted him; twice he met God and each time it came as a wound, and one time it came actually as a physical wound and he limped on his thigh for the rest of his life. And the man Elijah—was he not more than a theologian, more than a doctrinarian? He was a man who had been stricken; he had been struck with the sword of God and was no longer simply one of Adam's race standing up in his own self-assurance; he was a man who had had an encounter with God, who had been confronted by God and had been defeated and broken down before Him. And when Isaiah saw the Lord high and lifted up, you know what it did to him. Or take the man Ezekiel, how he went down before his God and became a little child again. And there were many others.

Now the wounded man is a defeated man, I say; the strong, robust and self-confident Adam-man ceases to fight back any longer; he lays down his sword and surrenders and the wound finishes him. Let's talk about these three wounds in their order.

The first is the wound of *contrition*. Now I've heard for the last thirty years that repentance is a change of mind, and I believe it, of course, as far as it goes. But that's just what's the matter with us. We have reduced repentance to a change of mind. It is a mental act, indeed, but I point out that repentance is not likely to do us much good until it ceases to be a change of mind only and becomes a wound within our spirit. No man has truly repented until his sin has wounded him near to death, until the wound has broken him and defeated him and taken all the fight and self-assurance out of him and he sees himself as the one who nailed his Savior on the tree.

I don't know about you, but the only way I can keep right with God is to keep contrite, to keep a sense of contrition upon my spirit. Now there's a lot of cheap and easy getting rid of sin and getting your repentance disposed of. But the great Christians, in and out of the Bible, have been those who were wounded with a sense of contrition so that they never quite got over the thought and the feeling that they personally had crucified Jesus. The great Bishop Ussher each week used to go down by the riverbank and there all Saturday afternoon kneel by a log and bewail his sins before his God. Perhaps that was the secret of his greatness.

Let us beware of vain and overhasty repentance, and particularly let us beware of no repentance at all. We are a sinful race, ladies and gentlemen, a sinful people, and until the knowledge has hit hard, until it has wounded us, until it has got through and past the little department of our theology, it has done us no good. A man can believe in total depravity and never have any sense of it for himself at all. Lots of us believe in total depravity who have never been wounded with the knowledge that we've sinned. Repentance is a wound I pray we may all feel.

And then there's the wound of *compassion*. Now compassion is an emotional identification, and Christ had that in full perfection. The man who has this wound of compassion is a man who suffers along with other people. Jesus Christ our Lord can never suffer to save us anymore. This He did, once for all, when He gave Himself without spot through the Holy Ghost to the Father on Calvary's cross. He cannot suffer to save us but He still must suffer to win us. He does not call His people to redemptive suffering. That's impossible; it could not be. Redemption is a finished work.

But He does call His people to feel along with Him and to feel along with those that rejoice and those that suffer. He calls His people to be to Him the kind of an earthly body in which He can weep again and suffer again and love again. For our Lord has two bodies. One is the body He took to the tree on Calvary; that was the body in which He suffered to redeem us. But He has a body on earth now, composed of those who have been baptized into it by the Holy Ghost at conversion. In that body He would now suffer to win men. Paul said that he was glad that he could suffer for the Colossians and fill up the measure of the afflictions of Christ in his body for the Church's sake.

Now, my brethren, I don't know whether I can make it clear or not. I know that things like this have to be felt rather than understood, but the wounded man is never a seeker after happiness. There is an ignoble pursuit of irresponsible happiness among us. Over the last years, as I have observed the human scene and have watched God's professed people live and die, I have seen that most of us would rather be happy than to feel the wounds of other people's sorrows. I do not believe that it is the will of God that we should seek to be happy, but rather that we should seek to be holy and useful. The holy man will be the useful man and he's likely to be a happy man too; but if he seeks happiness and forgets holiness and usefulness, he's a carnal man. I, for one, want no part in carnal religious joy. There are times when it's sinful to be happy. When Jesus our Lord was sweating it out there in the garden or hanging on the tree, He could not be happy. He was the "man of sorrows, and acquainted with grief" (Isaiah 53:3).

And the great saints of the past, who conquered and captured parts of the world for Jesus, when they were in travail were not happy. The woman, said Jesus, who is giving birth is not happy at the time of her travail, but as soon as the child is delivered she becomes happy because a man is born into the world. You and I are, in a sense, to be mothers in Israel, those through whom the Lord can suffer and grieve and love and pity again to bring children to birth.

Thirdly, there's the wound of *longing after God*. This little woman wanted to long after God with a longing that became a pain in her heart. She wanted to be lovesick. She prayed in effect, "O God, that I might want Thee so badly that it becomes a wound in my heart that I can't get over." Today, accepting Christ becomes terminal. That is the end. And all evangelism leads toward one thing—getting increased numbers of people to accept Christ, and there we put a period. My criticism of most of our Bible conferences is that we spend our time counting again the treasures that we have in Christ but we never arrive at the place where any of that which is in Christ gets into us. He has blessed us with all spiritual blessings in the heavenly places in Christ, but you can no more buy food with the money still in the bank than you can live on the treasures that are in Christ unless they're also experientially in you.

So many of us say, "All right, I'll attend another Bible conference," or "I'll take a course," or "I'll buy a book." My friends, what we need is not more instruction; we've been instructed to death. Where in the world is there more fundamental Bible teaching than here in Chicago? This is the Mecca of Fundamentalism. This is the Vatican of Evangelicalism. We've got notebooks at home stacked high that go back twenty-five years. They tell us of some new sidelight on some text or some new illustration somebody gave to point up a doctrine. But, oh, what weak creatures we are! What joyless people we are!

Note the paradoxes: to be happily forgiven and yet to be wounded and to remember the grief; to enjoy the peace of the finished work of Christ and yet suffer to win others; to find God and yet be always pursuing Him. When Moses saw the glory of God he begged that he might see more. When God revealed to him that he had found grace, he wanted more grace. Remember this: The man that has the most of God is the man who is seeking the most ardently for more of God.

There was a man who talked about "a restless thirst, a sacred, infinite desire," and that is what I want for my own heart. Among the plastic saints of our times Jesus has to do all the dying and all we want is to hear another sermon about His dying; Jesus does all the sorrowing and we want to be happy. But, my brethren, if we were what we ought to be, we would seek to know in experience the meaning of the words, "Except a corn of wheat fall into the ground and die, it abideth alone: but if it die, it bringeth forth much fruit" (John 12:24).

I have been greatly and deeply concerned that you and I do something more than listen, that we dare to go to God like the Lady Julian and dare to ask Him to give us a faithful, fatherly wound—maybe three of them, if you please: to wound us with a sense of our own sinful unworthiness that we'll never quite get over; to wound us with the sufferings of the world and the sorrows of the Church; and then to wound us with the longing after God, a thirst, a sacred thirst and longing that will carry us on toward perfection.

> *The lack of desire is the ill of all ills;*
>   *Many thousands through it the dark*
>   *pathway have trod;*
> *The balsam, the wine of predestinate wills*
>   *Is a jubilant pining and longing for God.* *

Write that sentence down, "A jubilant pining and longing for God."

Almost every day of my life I am praying that "a jubilant pining and longing for God" might come back on the evangelical churches. We don't need to have our doctrine straightened out; we're as orthodox as the Pharisees of old. But this longing for God that brings spiritual torrents and whirlwinds of seeking and self-denial—this is almost gone from our midst.

> *God loves to be longed for, He loves to be*
>   *sought,*
>   *For He sought us Himself with such longing*
>   *and love;*
> *He died for desire of us, marvelous thought!*
>   *And He longs for us now to be with Him*
>   *above.*

I believe that God wants us to long for Him with the longing that will become lovesickness, that will

* Frederick W. Faber

become a wound to our spirits, to keep us always moving toward Him, always finding and always seeking, always having and always desiring. So the earth becomes less and less valuable and heaven gets closer as we move into God and up into Christ.

Dare we bow our hearts now and say, "Father, I've been an irresponsible, childish kind of Christian—more concerned with being happy than with being holy. O God, give me three wounds. Wound me with a sense of my own sinfulness. Wound me with compassion for the world, and wound me with love of Thee that will keep me always pursuing and always exploring and always seeking and always finding."

If you dare to pray that prayer sincerely and mean it before God, it could mean a turning point in your life. It could mean a door of victory opened to you. May God grant that it be so.

Text of a sermon preached in Chicago 1953.

The Wrath of God: What Is It?

I t is rare that there is anything good in human anger. Almost always it springs out of unholy states of heart, and frequently it leads to cursing and violence. The man of evil temper is unpredictable and dangerous and is usually shunned by men of peace and good will.

There is a strong tendency among religious teachers these days to disassociate anger from the divine character and to defend God by explaining away the Scriptures that relate it to Him. This is understandable, but in the light of the full revelation of God it is inexcusable.

In the first place, God needs no defense. Those teachers who are forever trying to make God over in their own image might better be employed in seeking to make themselves over in the image of God. In the Scriptures "God spake all these words"

(Exodus 20:1), and there is no independent criterion by which we can judge the revelation God there makes concerning Himself.

The present refusal of so many to accept the doctrine of the wrath of God is part of a larger pattern of unbelief that begins with doubt concerning the veracity of the Christian Scriptures.

Let a man question the inspiration of the Scriptures and a curious, even monstrous, inversion takes place: thereafter he judges the Word instead of letting the Word judge him; he determines what the Word should teach instead of permitting it to determine what he should believe; he edits, amends, strikes out, adds at his pleasure; but always he sits above the Word and makes it amenable to him instead of kneeling before God and becoming amenable to the Word.

The tender-minded interpreter who seeks to shield God from the implications of His own Word is engaged in an officious effort that cannot but be completely wasted.

Why such a man still clings to the tattered relics of religion it is hard to say. The manly thing would be to walk out on the Christian faith and put it behind him along with other outgrown toys and discredited beliefs of childhood, but this he rarely does. He kills the tree but still hovers pensively about the orchard hoping for fruit that never comes.

Whatever is stated clearly but once in the Holy Scriptures may be accepted as sufficiently well established to invite the faith of all believers; and when we discover that the Spirit speaks of the wrath of God about 300 times in the Bible, we may as well make up our minds either to accept the doctrine or reject the Scriptures outright. If we have valid information from some outside source proving that anger is unworthy of God, then the Bible is not to be trusted when it attributes anger to God. And if it is wrong three hundred times on one subject, who can trust it on any other?

The instructed Christian knows that the wrath of God is a reality, that His anger is as holy as His love and that between His love and His wrath there is no incompatibility. He further knows (as far as fallen creatures can know such matters) what the wrath of God is and what it is not.

To understand God's wrath we must view it in the light of His holiness. God is holy and has made holiness to be the moral condition necessary to the health of His universe. Sin's temporary presence in the world only accents this. Whatever is holy is healthy; evil is a moral sickness that must end ultimately in death. The formation of the language itself suggests this, the English word *holy* deriving from the Anglo-Saxon *halig, hal* meaning *well, whole*. While it is not wise to press word origins unduly, there is yet a significance here that should not be overlooked.

Since God's first concern for His universe is its moral health, that is, its holiness, whatever is contrary to this is necessarily under His eternal displeasure. Wherever the holiness of God confronts unholiness there is conflict. This conflict arises from the irreconcilable natures of holiness and sin. God's attitude and action in the conflict are His anger. To preserve His creation God must destroy whatever would destroy it. When He arises to put down destruction and save the world from irreparable moral collapse He is said to be angry. Every wrathful judgment of God in the history of the world has been a holy act of preservation.

The holiness of God, the wrath of God and the health of the creation are inseparably united. Not only is it right for God to display anger against sin, but I find it impossible to understand how He could do otherwise.

God's wrath is His utter intolerance of whatever degrades and destroys. He hates iniquity as a mother hates the diphtheria or polio that would destroy the life of her child.

God's wrath is the antisepsis by which moral putrefaction is checked and the health of the creation maintained. When God warns of His impending wrath and exhorts men to repent and avoid it, He puts it in a language they can understand: He tells them to "flee from the wrath to come" (Luke 3:7). He says in effect, "Your life is evil, and because it is evil you are an enemy to the moral health of My creation. I must extirpate whatever would destroy the world I love. Turn from evil before I rise up in wrath against you. I love you, but I hate the sin you love. Separate yourself from your evil ways before I send judgment upon you."

"O LORD . . . in wrath remember mercy" (Habakkuk 3:2).

In Praise of Dogmatism

I t is vital to any understanding of ourselves and our fellowmen that we believe what is written in the Scriptures about human society, that it is fallen, alienated from God and in rebellion against His laws.

In these days of togetherness when all men would brothers be for a' that, even the true Christian is hard put to it to believe what God has spoken about men and their relation to each other and to God; for what He has spoken is never complimentary to men.

There is plenty of good news in the Bible, but there is never any flattery or back-scratching. Seen one way, the Bible is a book of doom. It condemns all men as sinners and declares that the soul that sinneth shall die. Always it pronounces sentence against society before it offers mercy; and if we will not own the validity of the sentence we cannot admit the need for mercy.

The coming of Jesus Christ to the world has been so sentimentalized that it means now something utterly alien to the biblical teaching concerning it. Soft human pity has been substituted for God's mercy in the minds of millions, a pity that has long ago degenerated into self-pity. The blame for man's condition has been shifted to God, and Christ's dying for the world has been twisted into an act of penance on God's part. In the drama of redemption man is viewed as Miss Cinderella who has long been oppressed and mistreated, but now through the heroic deeds of earth's noblest Son is about to don her radiant apparel and step forth a queen.

This is humanism romantically tinted with Christianity, a humanism that takes sides with rebels and excuses those who by word, thought and deed would glorify fallen men and if possible overthrow the glorious high Throne in the heavens.

According to this philosophy, men are never really to blame for anything, the exception being the man who insists that men are indeed to blame for something. In this dim world of pious sentiment all religions are equal and any man who insists that salvation is by Jesus Christ alone is a bigot and a boor.

So we pool our religious light, which if the truth is told is little more than darkness visible; we discuss religion on television and in the press as a kind of game, much as we discuss art and philosophy, accepting as one of the ground rules of the game that there is no final test of truth and that the best religion is a composite of the best in all religions. So we have truth by majority vote and thus saith the Lord by common consent.

One characteristic of this sort of thing is its timidity. That religion may be very precious to some persons is admitted, but never important enough to cause division or risk hurting anyone's feelings. In all our discussions there must never be any trace of intolerance; but we obviously forget that the most fervent devotees of tolerance are invariably intolerant of everyone who speaks about God with certainty. And there must be no bigotry, which is the name given to spiritual assurance by those who do not enjoy it.

The desire to please may be commendable enough under certain circumstances, but when pleasing men means displeasing God it is an unqualified evil and should have no place in the Christian's heart. To be right with God has often meant to be in trouble with men. This is such a common truth that one hesitates to mention it, yet it appears to have been overlooked by the majority of Christians today.

There is a notion abroad that to win a man we must agree with him. Actually the exact opposite is true. G.K. Chesterton remarked that each generation has had to be converted by the man who contradicted it most. The man who is going in a wrong direction will never be set right by the affable religionist who falls into step beside him and goes the same way. Someone must place himself across the path and insist that the straying man turn around and go in the right direction.

There is of course a sense in which we are all in this terrible human mess together, and for this reason there are certain areas of normal activity where we can all agree. The Christian will not disagree merely to be different, but wherever the moral standards and religious views of society differ from the teachings of Christ he will disagree flatly. He will not admit the validity of human opinion when the Word of God is clear. Some things are not debatable; there is no other side to them. There is only God's side.

When men believe God they speak boldly. When they doubt they confer. Much current religious talk is but uncertainty rationalizing itself; and this they call "engaging in the contemporary dialogue." It is impossible to imagine Moses or Elijah so occupied.

All great Christian leaders have been dogmatic. To such men two plus two made four. Anyone who insisted upon denying it or suspending judgment upon it was summarily dismissed as frivolous. They were only interested in a meeting of minds if the minds agreed to meet on holy ground. We could use some gentle dogmatists these days.

What Men Live By

Human life has its central core where lie the things men live by. These things are constant. They change not from age to age, but are the same among all races throughout the world always.

Life also has its marginal zones where lie the things that are relatively unimportant. These change from generation to generation and vary from people to people.

It is at the central core that men are one, and it is on the marginal zones that they differ from each other. Yet the marginal things divide the peoples of the world radically and seriously. Most of the enmities of the earth have arisen from differences that did not matter basically; but because the people could not distinguish things men live by from things they live with, these enmities arose between them, and often led to persecutions, murders and bloody wars.

Were men everywhere to ignore the things that matter little or not at all and give serious attention to the few really important things, most of the walls that divide men would be thrown down at once and a world of endless sufferings ended.

What does matter after all? What are the great facts that are good all the time everywhere among all men? What are the axiomatic truths upon which all human life may rest with confidence? Fortunately they are not many. Here are the chief ones:

1. *Only God is great.* Men have sought to place greatness elsewhere, in things, in events, in men; but the human soul is too great to attribute greatness to itself, and certainly too great to believe that things or events can possess true greatness.

The greatness that men seem to have is as the greatness of moonlight, which is but the glory of the sun reflected. Man's glory is borrowed. He shines in the light that never was on land or sea. He reflects God's greatness but has none of his own.

> *Before Thy ever-blazing throne*
> *We ask no luster of our own.*

2. *Only God is wise.* Man's wisdom has ever been the badge of his superiority and the cause of his most arrogant pride; yet it fails him constantly. He cannot by his wisdom find the answer to the old questions concerning himself: Whence? What? Why? Whither? By it he cannot secure the blessings he wants most: to escape pain, to stay young and to stay alive.

Yet man boasts of his wisdom. God waits, the ages pass, and time and space and matter and motion and life and death join to tell us that only God is wise.

3. _Apart from God nothing matters._ We think that health matters, that freedom matters or knowledge or art or civilization. And but for one insistent word they would matter indeed. That word is _eternity._

Grant that men possess perpetual being, and the preciousness of every earthly treasure is gone instantly. God is to our eternal being what our heart is to our body. The lungs, the liver, the kidneys have value as they relate to the heart. Let the heart stop and the rest of the organs promptly collapse. Apart from God, what is money, fame, education, civilization? Exactly nothing at all, for men must leave all these things behind them and one by one go to eternity. Let God hide His face and nothing thereafter is worth the effort.

4. _Only what we do in God will remain to us at last._ Man is made in the image of his Creator and has an urge toward creative activity. When he left the Garden his creative urge did not leave him. He must build, always build; his materials may be brick, paint, musical notes, scientific data, systems of thought; but always he must build, from the boy that builds a toy to the man that builds an empire.

Yet time is against him, for it wears out everything it touches. Its grinding action makes dust of civilizations and cities and men. A lifetime of toil dies with the toiler. But God puts immortality in all our loving efforts for Him and shares His eternity with all who love and trust Him.

5. *Human sin is real.* Suspicion, hate, envy, power, lust and greed keep the world in a state of continual ferment, while bespectacled men stand unblinking and assure classes of eager students that the whole idea of sin is outmoded and sin itself nonexistent.

In spite of all our smooth talk, sin continues to ride the race of man. Until its heavy weight is lifted from the soul, nothing else has any right to our attention, for sin shuts us out from the presence of the God whose favor alone gives life any satisfactory reason for being.

6. *With God there is forgiveness.* "The LORD God, merciful and gracious . . . keeping mercy for thousands, forgiving iniquity and transgression and sin." So says the Old Testament (Exodus 34:6-7). "The Son of man hath power on earth to forgive sins," says the New (Matthew 9:6).

God's mercy heads up in the Man Christ Jesus who is God and man by the mystery of the Incarnation. He can and does forgive sin because the sin was committed against Him in the first place. The soul in Christ has found the One that matters. His heaviest problem is solved; his basic philosophy is sound; his eyes are open and he knows the true from the false.

7. *Only what God protects is safe.* All else perishes with the using or the hoarding. Paul knew this secret. He said, "he is able to keep that which I have committed unto him against that day" (2 Timothy 1:12).

Blessed Treasure. Blessed Keeper. Blessed Day.

How to Try the Spirits

These are the times that try men's souls. The Spirit has spoken expressly that in the latter times some should depart from the faith, giving heed to seducing spirits and doctrines of demons; speaking lies in hypocrisy; having their consciences seared with a hot iron. Those days are upon us and we cannot escape them; we must triumph in the midst of them, for such is the will of God concerning us.

Strange as it may seem, the danger today is greater for the fervent Christian than for the lukewarm and the self-satisfied. The seeker after God's best things is eager to hear anyone who offers a way by which he can obtain them. He longs for some new experience, some elevated view of truth, some operation of the Spirit that will raise him above the dead level of religious mediocrity he sees all around him, and for this reason he is ready to give a sympathetic ear to the new and the wonderful in religion, particularly if it is presented by someone with an attractive personality and a reputation for superior godliness.

Now our Lord Jesus, that great Shepherd of the sheep, has not left His flock to the mercy of the wolves. He has given us the Scriptures, the Holy Spirit and natural powers of observation, and He expects us to avail ourselves of their help constantly. "Prove all things; hold fast that which is good," said Paul (1 Thessalonians 5:21). "Beloved, believe not every spirit," wrote John, "but try the spirits whether they are of God: because many false prophets are gone out into the world" (1 John 4:1). "Beware of false prophets," our Lord warned, "which come to you in sheep's clothing, but inwardly they are ravening wolves" (Matthew 7:15). Then He added the word by which they may be tested, "Ye shall know them by their fruits" (7:16).

From this it is plain not only that there shall be false spirits abroad, endangering our Christian lives, but that they may be identified and known for what they are. And of course once we become aware of their identity and learn their tricks, their power to harm us is gone. "Surely in vain the net is spread in the sight of any bird" (Proverbs 1:17).

It is my intention to set forth here a method by which we may test the spirits and prove all things religious and moral that come to us or are brought or offered to us by anyone. And while dealing with these matters we should keep in mind that not all religious vagaries are the work of Satan. The human mind is capable of plenty of mischief without any help from the devil. Some persons have a positive genius for getting confused and will mistake illusion for reality in broad daylight with the Bible open before them. Peter had such in mind when he wrote,

> Our beloved brother Paul also according to the wisdom given unto him hath written unto you; as also in all his epistles, speaking in them of these things; in which are some things hard to be understood, which they that are unlearned and unstable wrest, as they do also the other scriptures, unto their own destruction. (2 Peter 3:15-16)

It is unlikely that the confirmed apostles of confusion will read what is written here or that they would profit much if they did; but there are many sensible Christians who have been led astray but are humble enough to admit their mistakes and are now ready to return unto the Shepherd and Bishop of their souls. These may be rescued from false paths. More important still, there are undoubtedly large numbers of persons who have not left the true way but who want a rule by which they can test everything and by which they may prove the quality of Christian teaching and experience as they come in contact with them day after day throughout their busy lives. For such as these I make available here a little secret by which I have tested my own spiritual experiences and religious impulses for many years.

Briefly stated the test is this: This new doctrine, this new religious habit, this new view of truth, this new spiritual experience—*how has it affected my attitude toward and my relation to God, Christ, the Holy Scriptures, self, other Christians, the world and sin?* By this sevenfold test we may prove everything religious and know beyond a doubt whether it is of God or not. By the fruit of the tree we know the kind of tree it is. So we have but to ask about any doctrine or experience, what is this doing to me? and we know immediately whether it is from above or from below.

1. One vital test of all religious experience is how it affects our relation to God, our concept of God and our attitude toward Him.

God being who He is must always be the supreme arbiter of all things religious. The universe came into existence as a medium through which the Creator might show forth His perfections to all moral and intellectual beings: "I am the LORD: that is my name: and my glory will I not give to another" (Isaiah 42:8). "Thou art worthy, O Lord, to receive glory and honour and power: for thou hast created all things, and for thy pleasure they are and were created" (Revelation 4:11).

The health and balance of the universe require that in all things God should be magnified. "Great is the LORD, and greatly to be praised; and his greatness is unsearchable" (Psalm 145:3). God acts only for His glory and whatever comes from Him must be to His own high honor. Any doctrine, any experience that serves to magnify Him is likely to be inspired by Him. Conversely, anything that veils His glory or makes Him appear less wonderful is sure to be of the flesh or the devil.

The heart of man is like a musical instrument and may be played upon by the Holy Spirit, by an evil spirit or by the spirit of man himself. Religious emotions are very much the same, no matter who the player may be. Many enjoyable feelings may be aroused within the soul by low or even idolatrous worship. The nun who kneels "breathless with adoration" before an image of the virgin is having a genuine religious experience. She feels love, awe and reverence, all enjoyable emotions, as certainly as if she were adoring God. The mystical experiences of Hindus and Sufis cannot be brushed aside as mere pretense. Neither dare we dismiss the high religious flights of spiritists and other occultists as imagination. These may have and sometimes do have genuine encounters with something or someone beyond themselves. In the same manner Christians are sometimes led into emotional experiences that are beyond their power to comprehend. I have met such and they have inquired eagerly whether or not their experience was of God.

The big test is, What has this done to my relationship to the God and Father of our Lord Jesus Christ? If this new view of truth—this new encounter with spiritual things—has made me love God more, if it has magnified Him in my eyes, if it has purified my concept of His being and caused Him to appear more wonderful than before, then

I may conclude that I have not wandered astray into the pleasant but dangerous and forbidden paths of error.

2. The next test is, How has this new experience affected my attitude toward the Lord Jesus Christ? Whatever place present-day religion may give to Christ, God gives Him top place in earth and in heaven. "This is my beloved Son, in whom I am well pleased" (Matthew 3:17), spoke the voice of God from heaven concerning our Lord Jesus. Peter, full of the Holy Spirit, declared: "God hath made that same Jesus, whom ye have crucified, both Lord and Christ" (Acts 2:36). Jesus said of Himself, "I am the way, the truth, and the life: no man cometh unto the Father, but by me" (John 14:6). Again Peter said of Him, "Neither is there salvation in any other: for there is none other name under heaven given among men, whereby we must be saved" (Acts 4:12). The whole book of Hebrews is devoted to the idea that Christ is above all others. He is shown to be above Aaron and Moses, and even the angels are called to fall down and worship Him. Paul says that He is the image of the invisible God, that in Him dwells the fullness of the Godhead bodily and that in all things He must have the preeminence. But time would fail me to tell of the glory accorded Him by prophets, patriarchs, apostles, saints, elders, psalmists, kings and seraphim. He is made unto us wisdom and righteousness and sanctification and redemption. He is our hope, our life, our all and all, now and forevermore.

All this being true, it is clear that He must stand at the center of all true doctrine, all acceptable practice and all genuine Christian experience. Anything that makes Him less than God has declared Him to be is delusion pure and simple and must be rejected, no matter how delightful or how satisfying it may for the time seem to be.

Christless Christianity sounds contradictory but it exists as a real phenomenon in our day. Much that is being done in Christ's name is false to Christ in that it is conceived by the flesh, incorporates fleshly methods and seeks fleshly ends. Christ is mentioned from time to time in the same way and for the same reason that a self-seeking politician mentions Lincoln and the flag, to provide a sacred front for carnal activities and to deceive the simple-hearted listeners. This giveaway is that Christ is not central: He is not all and in all.

Again, there are psychic experiences that thrill the seeker and lead him to believe that he has indeed met the Lord and been carried to the third heaven; but the true nature of the phenomenon is discovered later when the face of Christ begins to fade from the victim's consciousness and he comes to depend more and more upon emotional jags as a proof of his spirituality.

If on the other hand the new experience tends to make Christ indispensable; if it takes our interest off our feeling and places it in Christ, we are on the right track. Whatever makes Christ dear to us is pretty sure to be from God.

3. Another revealing test of the soundness of religious experience is, How does it affect my attitude toward the Holy Scriptures?

Did this new experience, this new view of truth, spring out of the Word of God itself, or was it the result of some stimulus that lay outside the Bible? Tenderhearted Christians often become victims of strong psychological pressure applied intentionally or innocently by someone's personal testimony, or by a colorful story told by a fervent preacher who may speak with prophetic finality but who has not checked his story with the facts nor tested the soundness of his conclusions by the Word of God.

Whatever originates outside the Scriptures should for that very reason be suspect until it can be shown to be in accord with them. If it should be found to be contrary to the Word of revealed truth, no true Christian will accept it as being from God. However high the emotional content, no experience can be proved to be genuine unless we can find chapter and verse authority for it in the Scriptures. "To the word and to the testimony" must always be the last and final proof.

Whatever is new or singular should also be viewed with a lot of caution until it can furnish scriptural proof of its validity. Over the last half-century quite a number of unscriptural notions have gained acceptance among Christians by claiming that they were among the truths that were to be revealed in the last days. To be sure, say the advocates of this latter-day-light theory, Augustine did not know, Luther did not, John Knox, Wesley,

Finney and Spurgeon did not understand this; but greater light has now shined upon God's people and we of these last days have the advantage of fuller revelation. We should not question the new doctrine nor draw back from this advanced experience. The Lord is getting His Bride ready for the marriage supper of the Lamb. We should all yield to this new movement of the Spirit. So they tell us.

The truth is that the Bible does not teach that there will be new light and advanced spiritual experiences in the latter days; *it teaches the exact opposite*. Nothing in Daniel or the New Testament epistles can be tortured into advocating the idea that we of the end of the Christian era shall enjoy light that was not known at its beginning. Beware of any man who claims to be wiser than the apostles or holier than the martyrs of the Early Church. The best way to deal with him is to rise and leave his presence. You cannot help him and he surely cannot help you.

Granted, however, that the Scriptures may not always be clear and that there are differences of interpretation among equally sincere men, this test will furnish all the proof needed of anything religious, viz., What does it do to my love for and appreciation of the Scriptures?

While true power lies not in the letter of the text but in the Spirit that inspired it, we should never underestimate the value of the letter. The text of truth has the same relation to truth as the honeycomb has to honey. One serves as a receptacle for the other. But there the analogy ends. The honey can be removed from the comb, but the Spirit of truth cannot and does not operate apart from the letter of the Holy Scriptures. For this reason a growing acquaintance with the Holy Spirit will always mean an increasing love for the Bible. The Scriptures are in print what Christ is in person. The inspired Word is like a faithful portrait of Christ. But again the figure breaks down. Christ is in the Bible as no one can be in a mere portrait, for the Bible is a book of holy ideas and the eternal word of the Father can and does dwell in the thought He has Himself inspired. Thoughts are things, and the thoughts of the Holy Scriptures form a lofty temple for the dwelling place of God.

From this it follows naturally that a true lover of God will be also a lover of His Word. Anything that comes to us from the God of the Word will deepen our love for the Word of God. This follows logically, but we have confirmation by a witness vastly more trustworthy than logic, viz., the concerted testimony of a great army of witnesses living and dead. These declare with one voice that their love for the Scriptures intensified as their faith mounted and their obedience became consistent and joyous.

If the new doctrine, the influence of that new teacher, the new emotional experience fills my heart with an avid hunger to meditate in the Scriptures day and night, I have every reason to believe that God has spoken to my soul and that my experience is genuine. Conversely, if my love for the Scriptures has cooled even a little, if my eagerness to eat and drink of the inspired Word has abated by as much as one degree, I should humbly admit that I have missed God's signal somewhere and frankly backtrack until I find the true way once more.

4. Again, we can prove the quality of religious experience by its effect on the self-life.

The Holy Spirit and the fallen human self are diametrically opposed to each other. "The flesh lusteth against the Spirit, and the spirit against the flesh: and these are contrary the one to the other: so that ye cannot do the things that ye would" (Galatians 5:17). "They that are after the flesh do mind the things of the flesh; but they that are after the Spirit the things of the Spirit. . . . Because the carnal mind is enmity against God: for it is not subject to the law of God, neither indeed can be" (Romans 8: 5, 7).

Before the Spirit of God can work creatively in our hearts He must condemn and slay the "flesh" within us; that is, He must have our full consent to displace our natural self with the Person of Christ. This displacement is carefully explained in Romans 6, 7 and 8. When the seeking Christian has gone through the crucifying experience described in chapters 6 and 7 he enters into the broad, free regions of chapter 8. There self is dethroned and Christ is enthroned forever.

In the light of this it is not hard to see why the Christian's attitude toward self is such an excellent test of the validity of his religious experiences. Most of the great masters of the deeper life, such as Fénelon, Molinos, John of the Cross, Madame Guyon and a host of others, have warned against pseudoreligious experiences that provide much carnal enjoyment but feed the flesh and puff up the heart with self-love.

A good rule is this: If this experience has served to humble me and make me little and vile in my own eyes, it is of God; but if it has given me a feeling of self-satisfaction, it is false and should be dismissed as emanating from self or the devil. Nothing that comes from God will minister to my pride or self-congratulation. If I am tempted to be complacent and to feel superior because I have had a remarkable vision or an advanced spiritual experience, I should go at once to my knees and repent of the whole thing. I have fallen a victim to the enemy.

5. Our relation to and our attitude toward our fellow Christians is another accurate test of religious experience.

Sometimes an earnest Christian will, after some remarkable spiritual encounter, withdraw himself from his fellow believers and develop a spirit of faultfinding. He may be honestly convinced that his experience is superior, that he is now in an advanced state of grace, and that the hoi polloi in the church where he attends are but a mixed multitude and he alone a true son of Israel. He may struggle to be patient with these religious worldlings, but his soft language and condescending smile reveal his true opinion of them—and of himself. This is a dangerous state of mind, and the more dangerous because it can justify itself by the facts. The brother *has* had a remarkable experience; he *has* received some wonderful light on the Scriptures; he *has* entered into a joyous land unknown to him before. And it may easily be true that the professed Christians with whom he is acquainted are worldly and dull and without spiritual enthusiasm. It is not that he is mistaken in his facts that proves him to be in error, but that his reaction to the facts is of the flesh. His new spirituality has made him less charitable.

The Lady Julian tells us in her quaint English how true Christian grace affects our attitude toward others: "For of all things the beholding and loving of the Maker maketh the soul to seem less in his own sight, and most filleth him with reverent dread and true meekness; with plenty of charity to his fellow Christians." Any religious experience that fails to deepen our love for our fellow Christians may safely be written off as spurious.

The apostle John makes love for our fellow Christians to be a test of true faith. "My little children, let us not love in word, neither in tongue; but in deed and in truth. And hereby we know that we are of the truth, and shall assure our hearts before him" (1 John 3:18-19). Again he says, "Beloved, let us love one another: for love is of God; and every one that loveth is born of God, and knoweth God. He that loveth not knoweth not God; for God is love" (1 John 4: 7-8).

As we grow in grace we grow in love toward all God's people. "Every one that loveth him that begat loveth him also that is begotten of him" (1 John 5:1). This means simply that if we love God we will love

His children. All true Christian experience will deepen our love for other Christians.

Therefore we conclude that whatever tends to separate us in person or in heart from our fellow Christians is not of God, but is of the flesh or of the devil. And conversely, whatever causes us to love the children of God is likely to be of God. "By this shall all men know that ye are my disciples, if ye have love one to another" (John 13:35).

6. Another certain test of the source of religious experience is this: Note how it affects our relation to and our attitude toward the world.

By "the world" I do not mean, of course, the beautiful order of nature which God has created for the enjoyment of mankind. Neither do I mean the world of lost men in the sense used by our word when He said, "God so loved the world, that he gave his only begotten Son, that whosoever believeth in him should not perish, but have everlasting life. For God sent not his Son into the world to condemn the world; but that the world through him might be saved" (John 3:16-17). Certainly any true touch of God in the soul will deepen our appreciation of the beauties of nature and intensify our love for the lost. I refer here to something else altogether.

Let an apostle say it for us: "All that is in the world, the lust of the flesh, and the lust of the eyes, and the pride of life, is not of the Father, but is of the world. And the world passeth away, and the lust thereof: but he that doeth the will of God abideth for ever" (1 John 2:16-17).

This is the world by which we may test the spirits. It is the world of carnal enjoyments, of godless pleasures, of the pursuit of earthly riches and reputation and sinful happiness. It carries on without Christ, following the counsel of the ungodly and being animated by "the prince of the power of the air, the spirit that now worketh in the children of disobedience" (Ephesians 2:2). Its religion is a form of godliness, without power, which has a name to live but is dead. It is, in short, unregenerate human society romping on its way to hell, the exact opposite of the true Church of God, which is a society of regenerate souls going soberly but joyfully on their way to heaven.

Any real work of God in our hearts will tend to unfit us for the world's fellowship. "Love not the world, neither the things that are in the world. If any man love the world, the love of the Father is not in him" (1 John 2:15). "Be ye not unequally yoked together with unbelievers: for what fellowship hath righteousness with unrighteousness? and what communion hath light with darkness?" (2 Corinthians 6:14). It may be stated unequivocally that any spirit that permits compromise with the world is a false spirit. Any religious movement that imitates the world in any of its manifestations is false to the cross of Christ and on the side of the devil—and this regardless of how much purring its leaders may do about "accepting Christ" or "letting God run your business."

7. The last test of the genuineness of Christian experience is what it does to our attitude toward sin.

The operations of grace within the heart of a believing man will turn that heart away from sin and toward holiness,

> For the grace of God that bringeth salvation hath appeared to all men, teaching us that, denying ungodliness and worldly lusts, we should live soberly, righteously, and godly, in this present world; looking for that blessed hope, and the glorious appearing of the great God and our Saviour Jesus Christ. (Titus 2:11-13)

I do not see how it could be plainer. The same grace that saves teaches that saved man inwardly, and its teaching is both negative and positive. Negatively it teaches us to deny ungodliness and worldly lusts. Positively it teaches us to live soberly, righteously and godly right in this present world.

The man of honest heart will find no difficulty here. He has but to check his own bent to discover whether he is concerned about sin in his life more or less since the supposed work of grace was done. Anything that weakens his hatred of sin may be identified immediately as false to the Scriptures, to the Savior and to his own soul. Whatever makes holiness more attractive and sin more intolerable may be accepted as genuine. "For thou art not a God that hath pleasure in wickedness: neither shall evil dwell with thee. The foolish shall not stand in thy sight: thou hatest all workers of iniquity" (Psalm 5:4-5).

Jesus warned, "There shall arise false Christs, and false prophets, and shall shew great signs and wonders; insomuch that, if it were possible, they shall deceive the very elect" (Matthew 24:24). These words describe our day too well to be coincidental. In the hope that the "elect" may profit by them I have set forth these tests. The result is in the hand of God.

Religious Boredom

That there is something gravely wrong with evangelical Christianity today is not likely to be denied by any serious-minded person acquainted with the facts. Just *what* is wrong is not so easy to determine.

In examining the situation myself I find nature and reason in conflict within me, for I tend by temperament to want to settle everything with a sweep of the pen. But reason advises caution; nothing is that simple, and we must be careful to distinguish cause from effect. As every doctor knows there is a wide difference between the disease and the symptoms; and every Christian knows that there is a big difference between cause and effect in the sphere of religion.

At the root of our spiritual trouble lies a number of causes and these causes have effects, but which is cause and which is effect is not always known. I suspect that many things currently under attack by our evangelists and pastors (and editors, for that matter) are not the causes of our troubles but the effects of causes that lie deeper. We treat the symptoms and wonder why the patient does not get well. Or, to change the figure, we lay down a heavy fire against nothing more substantial than the cloud of dust raised by marching enemy troops long gone by.

One mark of the low state of affairs among us is religious boredom. Whether this is a thing in itself or merely a symptom of the thing, I do not know for sure, though I suspect that it is the latter. And that it is found to some degree almost everywhere among Christians is too evident to be denied.

Boredom is, of course, a state of mind resulting from trying to maintain an interest in something that holds no trace of interest for us (the boss's jokes, say, or that lecture on the care and nurture of dahlias to which we went because we could not resist the enthusiastic urging of a friend). No one is bored by what he can in good conscience walk away from. Boredom comes when a man must try to hear with relish what for want of relish he hardly hears at all.

By this definition there is certainly much boredom in religion these days. The businessman on a Sunday morning whose mind is on golf can scarcely disguise his lack of interest in the sermon he is compelled to hear. The housewife who is unacquainted with the learned theological or philosophical jargon of the speaker; the young couple who feel a tingle of love for each other but who neither love nor know the One about whom the choir is singing—these cannot escape the low-grade mental pain we call boredom while they struggle to keep their attention focused upon the service. All these are too courteous to admit to others that they are bored and possibly too timid to admit it even to themselves, but I believe that a bit of candid confession would do us all good.

When Moses tarried in the mount, Israel became bored with the faith that sees the invisible and clamored for a god they could see and touch. And they displayed a great deal more enthusiasm for the golden calf than they did over the Lord God of Abraham. Later they tired of manna and complained against the monotony of their diet. On their petulant insistence they finally got flesh to eat; and that to their own undoing.

Those Christians who belong to the evangelical wing of the Church (which I firmly believe is the only one that even approximates New Testament Christianity) have over the last half-century shown an increasing impatience with things invisible and eternal and have demanded and got a host of things visible and temporal to satisfy their fleshly appetites. Without biblical authority, or any other right under the sun, carnal religious leaders have introduced a host of attractions that serve no purpose except to provide entertainment for the retarded saints.

It is now common practice in most evangelical churches to offer the people, especially the young people, a maximum of entertainment and a minimum of serious instruction. It is scarcely possible in most places to get anyone to attend a meeting where the only attraction is God. One can only conclude that God's professed children are bored with Him, for they must be wooed to meeting with a stick of striped candy in the form of religious movies, games and refreshments.

This has influenced the whole pattern of church life, and even brought into being a new type of church architecture, designed to house the golden calf.

So we have the strange anomaly of orthodoxy in creed and heterodoxy in practice. The striped-candy technique has been so fully integrated into our present religious thinking that it is simply taken for granted. Its victims never dream that it is not a part of the teachings of Christ and His apostles.

Any objection to the carryings on of our present golden-calf Christianity is met with the triumphant reply, "But we are winning them!" And winning them to what? To true discipleship? To cross-carrying? To self-denial? To separation from the world? To crucifixion of the flesh? To holy living? To nobility of character? To a despising of the world's treasures? To hard self-discipline? To love for God? To total committal to Christ? Of course the answer to all these questions is *no*.

We are paying a frightful price for our religious boredom. And that at the moment of the world's mortal peril.

CHAPTER

31

The Church Cannot Die

There is a notion abroad that Christianity is on its last legs, or possibly already dead and just too weak to lie down.

This is confidently believed in communist countries, and while spokesmen for the West are too polite to say so, one can hardly escape the feeling that they too believe the demise of the Church to be a certain if embarrassing fact, the chief proof of her death being her failure to provide leadership for the world just when it needs it most.

Let me employ a pair of mixed and battered but still useful clichés and say that those who have come to bury the faith of our fathers have reckoned without the host. Just as Jesus Christ was once buried away with the full expectation that He had been gotten rid of, so His Church has been laid to rest times without number; and as He disconcerted His enemies by rising from the dead so the Church has confounded hers by springing again to vigorous life after all the obsequies had been performed over her coffin and the crocodile tears had been shed at her grave.

The language of devotion has helped to create the impression that the Church is supposed to be a band of warriors driving the enemy before them in plain sight and with plenty of color and drama to give a pleasing flourish to the whole thing. In our hymns and pulpit oratory we have commonly pictured the Church as marching along to the sound of martial music and the plaudits of the multitude.

Of course this is but a poetic figure. The individual Christian may be likened to a soldier, but the picture of the Church on earth as a conquering army is not realistic. Her true situation is more accurately portrayed as a flock of sheep in the midst of wolves, or as a company of despised pilgrims plodding toward home, or as a peculiar nation protected by the Passover blood waiting for the sound of the trumpet, or as a bride looking for the coming of her bridegroom.

The world is constantly lashing the Church because she has no solution for the problems of society, and the religious leaders who do not know the score wince under the lash. Every once in a while some churchman in an acute attack of conscience does penance in public for Christianity's failure to furnish bold leadership for the world in this time of crisis. "We have sinned," cries the frustrated prophet. "The world looked to us for help and we have failed it."

Well, I am all for repentance if it is genuine, and I think the Church *has* failed, not by neglecting to provide leadership but by living too much like the world. That, however, is not what the muddled churchman means when he bares his soul in public. Rather, he erroneously assumes that the Church of God has been left on earth to minister good hope and cheer to the world in such quantities that it can ignore God, reject Christ, glorify fallen human flesh and pursue its selfish ends in peace. The world wants the Church to add a dainty spiritual touch to its carnal schemes and to be there to help it to its feet and put it to bed when it comes home drunk with fleshly pleasures.

In the first place the Church has received no such commission from her Lord, and in the second place the world has never shown much disposition to listen to the Church when she speaks in her true prophetic voice. The attitude of the world toward the true child of God is precisely the same as that of the citizens of Vanity Fair toward Christian and his companion, "Therefore they took them and beat them, and besmeared them with dirt, and put them into the cage, that they might be made a spectacle to all men." Christian's duty was not to "provide leadership" for Vanity Fair but to keep clean from its pollution and get out of it as fast as possible. He that hath ears to hear, let him hear.

Christianity is going the way her Founder and His apostles said it would go. Its development and direction were predicted almost two thousand years ago, and this itself is a miracle. Had Christ been less than God and His apostles less than inspired, they could not have foretold with such precision the state of the Church so far removed from them in time and circumstance. No mortal man could have foreseen the coming of the great religio-political system that is Rome, or the Dark Ages, or the discovery of the New World, or the Industrial Revolution and the rise of higher criticism, or the nuclear age and man's adventure into space. All these would have upset any human effort to foretell the religious situation these latter days; but present conditions were in fact depicted in great fullness of detail nearly two thousand years ago. Nothing unexpected has happened or is happening.

We are in real need of a reformation that will lead to revival among the churches, but the Church is not dead, neither is it dying. The Church cannot die. A local church can die. This happens when all the old saints in a given place fall asleep and no young saints arise to take their place. Sometimes under these circumstances the congregation ceases to be a church, or there is no congregation left and the doors of the chapel are nailed shut. But such a condition, however deplorable, should not discourage us. The true Church is the repository of the life of God among men, and if in one place the frail vessels fail, that life will break out somewhere else. Of this we may be sure.

CHAPTER

32

The Lordship of the Man Jesus Is Basic

We are under constant temptation these days to substitute another Christ for the Christ of the New Testament. The whole drift of modern religion is toward such a substitution.

To avoid this we must hold steadfastly to the concept of Christ as set forth so clearly and plainly in the Scriptures of truth. Though an angel from heaven should preach anything less than the Christ of the apostles, let him be forthrightly and fearlessly rejected.

The mighty, revolutionary message of the Early Church was that a man named Jesus who had been crucified was now raised from the dead and exalted to the right hand of God. "Therefore let all the house of Israel know assuredly, that God hath made that same Jesus, whom ye have crucified, both Lord and Christ" (Acts 2:36).

Less than three hundred years after Pentecost the hard-pressed defenders of the faith drew up a manifesto condensing those teachings of the New Testament having to do with the nature of Christ. This manifesto declares that Christ is

> God of the substance of His Father, begotten before all ages: Man of the substance of His mother, born in the world: perfect God and perfect Man, of a reasonable soul and human flesh subsisting: Equal to His Father, as touching His Godhead: less than the Father, as touching His manhood. Who, although He be God and man, yet He is not two, but one Christ. One, not by conversion of the Godhead into flesh, but by the taking of the manhood into God. One altogether, not by the confusion of substance, but by the unity of Person. For as the reasonable soul and flesh is one man, so God and man is one Christ.

Even among those who acknowledge the deity of Christ there is often a failure to recognize His manhood. We are quick to assert that when He walked the earth He was *God with men*, but we overlook a truth equally as important, that where He sits now on His mediatorial throne He is *Man with God*.

The teaching of the New Testament is that now, at this very moment, there is a man in heaven appearing in the presence of God for us. He is as certainly a man as was Adam or Moses or Paul. He is a man glorified, but His glorification did not dehumanize Him. Today He is a real man, of the race of mankind, bearing our lineaments and dimensions, a visible and audible man whom any other man would recognize instantly as one of us.

But more than this, He is heir of all things, Lord of all worlds, head of the Church and the first-born of the new creation. He is the way to God, the life of the believer, the hope of Israel and the High Priest of every true worshiper. He holds the keys of death and hell and stands as advocate and surety for everyone who believes on Him in truth.

This is not all that can be said about Him, for were all said that might be said I suppose the world itself could not contain the books that should be written. But this in brief is the Christ we preach to sinners as their only escape from the wrath to come. With Him rest the noblest hopes and dreams of men. All the longings for immortality that rise and swell in the human breast will be fulfilled in Him or they will never know fulfillment. There is no other way (John 14:6).

Salvation comes not by "accepting the finished work" or "deciding for Christ." It comes by believing on the Lord Jesus Christ, the whole, living, victorious Lord who, as God and man, fought our fight and won it, accepted our debt as His own and paid it, took our sins and died under them and rose again to set us free. This is the true Christ, and nothing less will do.

But something less is among us, nevertheless, and we do well to identify it so that we may repudiate it. That something is a poetic fiction, a product of the romantic imagination and maudlin religious fancy. It is a Jesus, gentle, dreamy, shy, sweet, almost effeminate and marvelously adaptable to whatever society He may find Himself in. He is cooed over by women disappointed in love, patronized by pro tem celebrities and recommended by psychiatrists as a model of a well-integrated personality. He is used as a means to almost any carnal end, but He is never acknowledged as Lord. These quasi-Christians follow a quasi-Christ. They want His help but not His interference. They will flatter Him but never obey Him.

The argument of the apostles is that the Man Jesus has been made higher than angels, higher than Moses and Aaron, higher than any creature in earth or heaven. And this exalted position He attained *as a man*. As God He already stood infinitely above all other beings. No argument was needed to prove the transcendence of the Godhead. The apostles were not declaring the preeminence of God, which would have been superfluous, but of a man, which was necessary. Those first Christians believed that Jesus of Nazareth, a man they knew, had been raised to a position of Lordship over the universe. He was still their friend, still one of them, but had left them for a while to appear in the presence of God on their behalf. And the proof of this was the presence of the Holy Spirit among them.

One cause of our moral weakness today is an inadequate Christology. We think of Christ as God but fail to conceive of Him as a man glorified. To recapture the power of the Early Church we must believe what they believed. And they believed they had a God-approved Man representing them in heaven.

A Do-It-Yourself Education Is Better Than None

This is written for those Christians who may have missed a formal education. Let no one despair. A do-it-yourself education is better than none. It can be acquired by the proper use of our mental powers.

Our intellectual activities in the order of their importance may be graded this way: first, cogitation; second, observation; third, reading.

I wish I could include conversation in this short list. One would naturally suppose that verbal intercourse with congenial friends should be one of the most profitable of all mental activities; and it may have been so once but no more. It is now quite possible to talk for hours with civilized men and women and gain absolutely nothing from it. Conversation today is almost wholly sterile. Should the talk start on a fairly high level, it is sure within a few minutes to degenerate into cheap gossip, shoptalk, banter, weak humor, stale jokes, puns and second-hand quips. So we shall omit conversation from our list of useful intellectual activities, at least until there has been a radical reformation in the art of social discourse.

We shall not consider prayer here either, but for quite another and happier reason. Prayer is the loftiest activity possible to man, and it is of course partly mental, but it is nevertheless usually classified as a spiritual rather than an intellectual exercise; so it will be omitted.

I believe that pure thinking will do more to educate a man than any other activity he can engage in. To afford sympathetic entertainment to abstract ideas, to let one idea beget another, and that another, till the mind teems with them; to compare one idea with others, to weigh, to consider, evaluate, approve, reject, correct, refine; to join thought with thought like an architect till a noble edifice has been created within the mind; to travel back in imagination to the beginning of the creation and then to leap swiftly forward to the end of time; to bound upward through illimitable space and downward into the nucleus of an atom; and all this without so much as moving from our chair or opening the eyes—this is to soar above all the lower creation and to come near to the angels of God.

Of all earth's creatures only man can think in this way. And while thinking is the mightiest act a man can perform, perhaps for the very reason that it is the mightiest, it is the one act he likes the least and avoids most.

Aside from a few professionals, who cannot number more than one-tenth of one percent of the population, people simply do not think at all except in the most elementary way. Their thinking is done for them by the professionals.

After cogitation comes observation (in order of importance, not in order of time). Observation is, of course, simply a method of obtaining information. Without information the most powerful mind can produce nothing worthwhile. Philosophers have not agreed about whether the mind receives all of its ideas through the five senses or comes into the world with a few "innate ideas," i.e., ideas already present. But we need not settle this argument to conclude that information is indispensable to sound thought. Knowledge is the raw material out of which that finest of all machines, the mind, creates its amazing world.

The effort to think well with an empty head is sure to be largely wasted. There is nothing like a good hard fact to correct our carefully constructed theories. God has given us our five senses, and these are most highly sensitive instruments for the gathering of knowledge. So efficient are these instruments that it is quite impossible for a normal person to live even a brief time without learning something. For this reason a child five years old may properly be said to be educated in that he has by observation gathered a few facts and arranged them into some sort of orderly pattern within his mind. A doctor of philosophy has done nothing different; he has only gone a little further.

While it is impossible to live even a short time without learning something, unfortunately it is possible to live a long time and not learn very much. Observation is a powerful tool, but its usefulness depends upon how well we use it. One of the tragedies of life is that the powers of observation atrophy when not used. Just when this begins with the average person I have no sure way of knowing, but I would hazard a guess that it is at about the age of twenty-five. By that time most people have formed their habits, accepted the conventions, lost their sense of wonder and settled down to live by their glands and their appetites. For millions there is not much to observe after that but the weather and the baseball score.

Lastly, reading. To think without a proper amount of good reading is to limit our thinking to our own tiny plot of ground. The crop cannot be large. To observe only and neglect reading is to deny ourselves the immense value of other people's observations; and since the better books are written by trained observers the loss is sure to be enormous. Extensive reading without the discipline of practical observation will lead to bookishness and artificiality. Reading and observing without a great deal of meditating will fill the mind with learned lumber that will always remain alien to us. Knowledge to be our own must be digested by thinking.

Some Thoughts on Books and Reading

One big problem in many parts of the world today is to learn how to read, and in others it is to find something to read after one has learned. In our favored West we are overwhelmed with printed matter, so the problem here becomes one of selection. We must decide what not to read.

Nearly a century ago Emerson pointed out that if it were possible for a man to begin to read the day he was born and to go on reading without interruption for seventy years, at the end of that time he would have read only enough books to fill a tiny niche in the British Library. Life is so short and the books available to us are so many that no man can possibly be acquainted with more than a fraction of one percent of the books published.

It hardly need be said that most of us are not selective enough in our reading. I have often wondered how many square yards of newsprint passes in front of the eyes of the average civilized man in the course of a year. Surely it must run into several acres; and I am afraid our average reader does not realize a very large crop on his acreage. The best advice I have heard on this topic was given by a Methodist minister. He said, "Always read your newspaper standing up." Henry David Thoreau also had a low view of the daily press. Just before leaving the city for his now-celebrated sojourn on the banks of Walden Pond a friend asked him if he would like to have a newspaper delivered to his cottage. "No," replied Thoreau, "I have already seen a newspaper."

In our serious reading we are likely to be too greatly influenced by the notion that the chief value of a book is to inform; and if we were talking of textbooks of course that would be true, but when we speak or write of books we have not textbooks in mind.

The best book is not one that informs merely, but one that stirs the reader up to inform himself. The best writer is one that goes with us through the world of ideas like a friendly guide who walks beside us through the forest pointing out to us a hundred natural wonders we had not noticed before. So we learn from him to see for ourselves and soon we have no need for our guide. If he has done his work well we can go on alone and miss little as we go.

That writer does the most for us who brings to our attention thoughts that lay close to our minds waiting to be acknowledged as our own. Such a man acts as a midwife to assist at the birth of ideas that had been gestating long within our souls, but which without his help might not have been born at all. There are few emotions so satisfying as the joy that comes from the act of recognition when we see and identify our own thoughts. We have all had teachers who sought to educate us by feeding alien ideas into our minds, ideas for which we felt no spiritual or intellectual kinship. These we dutifully tried to integrate into our total spiritual philosophy but always without success.

In a very real sense no man can teach another; he can only aid him to teach himself. Facts can be transferred from one mind to another as a copy is made from the master tape on a sound recorder. History, science, even theology, may be taught in this way, but it results in a highly artificial kind of learning and seldom has any good effect upon the deep life of the student. What the learner contributes to the learning process is fully as important as anything contributed by the teacher. If nothing is contributed by the learner the results are useless; at best there will be but the artificial creation of another teacher who can repeat the dreary work on someone else, ad infinitum.

Perception of ideas rather than the storing of them should be the aim of education. The mind should be an eye to see with rather than a bin to store facts in. The man who has been taught by the Holy Spirit will be a seer rather than a scholar. The difference is that the scholar sees and the seer sees through; and that is a mighty difference indeed.

The human intellect even in its fallen state is an awesome work of God, but it lies in darkness until it has been illuminated by the Holy Spirit. Our Lord has little good to say of the unilluminated mind, but He revels in the mind that has been renewed and enlightened by grace. He always makes the place of His feet glorious; there is scarcely anything on earth more beautiful than a Spirit-filled mind, certainly nothing more wonderful than an alert and eager mind made incandescent by the presence of the indwelling Christ.

Since what we read in a real sense enters the soul, it is vitally important that we read the best and nothing but the best. I cannot but feel that Christians were better off before there was so much reading matter to choose from. Today we must practice sharp discipline in our reading habits. Every Christian should master the Bible, or at least spend hours and days and years trying. And always he should read his Bible, as George Müller said, "with meditation."

After the Bible the next most valuable book for the Christian is a *good* hymnal. Let any young Christian spend a year prayerfully meditating on the hymns of Watts and Wesley alone and he will become a fine theologian. Then let him read a balanced diet of the Puritans and the Christian mystics. The results will be more wonderful than he could have dreamed.

CHAPTER

35

The Decline of
Apocalyptic Expectation

A short generation ago, or about the time of the first World War, there was a feeling among gospel Christians that the end of the age was near, and many were breathless with anticipation of a new world order about to emerge.

This new order was to be preceded by a silent return of Christ to earth, not to remain, but to raise the righteous dead to immortality and to glorify the living saints in the twinkling of an eye. These He would catch away to the marriage supper of the Lamb, while the earth meanwhile plunged into its baptism of fire and blood in the Great Tribulation. This would be relatively brief, ending dramatically with the battle of Armageddon and the triumphant return of Christ with His Bride to reign a thousand years.

Thus the hopes and dreams of Christians were directed toward an event to be followed by a new order in which they would have a leading part. This expectation for many was so real that it quite literally determined their world outlook and way of life. One well-known and highly respected Christian leader, when handed a sum of money to pay off the mortgage on the church building, refused to use it for that purpose. Instead he used it to help send missionaries to the heathen to hasten the Lord's return. This is probably an extreme example, but it does reveal the acute apocalyptic expectation that prevailed among Christians around the time of World War I and immediately following.

Before we condemn this as extravagant we should back off a bit and try to see the whole thing in perspective. We may be wiser now (though that is open to serious question), but those Christians had something very wonderful which we today lack. They had a unifying hope; we have none. Their activities were concentrated; ours are scattered, overlapping and often self-defeating. They fully expected to win; we are not even sure we know what "win" means. Our Christian hope has been subjected to so much examination, analysis and revision that we are embarrassed to admit that we have such a hope at all.

And those expectant believers were not wholly wrong. They were only wrong about the time. They saw Christ's triumph as being nearer than it was, and for that reason their timing was off; but their hope itself was valid. Many of us have had the experience of misjudging the distance of a mountain toward which we were traveling. The huge bulk that loomed against the sky seemed very near, and it was hard to persuade ourselves that it was not receding as we approached. So the City of God appears so large to the minds of the world-weary pilgrim that he is sometimes the innocent victim of an optical illusion; and he may be more than a little disappointed when the glory seems to move farther away as he approaches.

But the mountain is there; the traveler need only press on to reach it. And the Christian's hope is there too; his judgment is not always too sharp, but he is not mistaken in the long view; he will see the glory in God's own time.

We evangelicals have become sophisticated, blasé. We have lost what someone called the "millennial component" from our Christian faith. To escape what we believe to be the slough of a mistaken hope we have detoured far out into the wilderness of complete hopelessness.

Christians now chatter learnedly about things simple believers have always taken for granted. They are on the defensive, trying to prove things that a previous generation never doubted. We have allowed unbelievers to get us in a corner and have given them the advantage by permitting them to choose the time and place of encounter. We smart under the attack of the quasi-Christian unbeliever, and the nervous, self-conscious defense we make is called "the religious dialogue."

Under the scornful attack of the religious critic real Christians who ought to know better are now "rethinking" their faith. Scarcely anything has escaped the analysts. With a Freudian microscope they examine everything: foreign missions, the book of Genesis, the inspiration of the Scriptures, morals, all tried and proven methods, polygamy, liquor, sex, prayer—all have come in for inquisition by those who engage in the contemporary dialogue. Adoration has given way to celebration in the holy place, if indeed any holy place remains to this generation of confused Christians. The causes of the decline of apocalyptic expectation are many, not the least being the affluent society in which we live. If the rich man with difficulty enters the kingdom of God, then it would be logical to conclude that a society having the highest percentage of well-to-do persons in it would have the lowest percentage of Christians, all things else being equal. If the "deceitfulness of riches" chokes the Word and makes it unfruitful, then this would be the day of near-fruitless preaching, at least in the opulent West. And if surfeiting and drunkenness and worldly cares tend to unfit the Christian for the coming of Christ, then this generation of Christians should be the least prepared for that event.

On the North American continent Christianity has become the religion of the prosperous middle and upper classes almost entirely, the very rich or the very poor rarely become practicing Christians. The touching picture of the poorly dressed, hungry saint, clutching his Bible under his arm and with the light of God shining in his face hobbling painfully toward the church, is chiefly imaginary. One of the biggest problems of even the most ardent Christian these days is to find a parking place for the shiny chariot that transports him effortlessly to the house of God where he hopes to prepare his soul for the world to come.

In the United States and Canada the middle class today possesses more earthly goods and lives in greater luxury than emperors and maharajahs did a short century ago. And since the bulk of Christians comes from this class it is not difficult to see why the apocalyptic hope has all but disappeared from among us. It is hard to focus attention upon a better world to come when a more comfortable one than this can hardly be imagined. The best we can do is to look for heaven after we have reveled for a lifetime in the luxuries of a fabulously generous earth. As long as science can make us so cozy in this present world, it is hard to work up much pleasurable anticipation of a new world order.

But affluence is only one cause of the decline of the apocalyptic hope. There are other and more important ones.

The whole problem is a big one, a theological one, a moral one. An inadequate view of Christ may be the chief trouble. Christ has been explained, humanized, demoted. Many professed Christians no longer expect Him to usher in a new order; they are not at all sure that He is able to do so; or if He does, it will be with the help of art, education, science and technology; that is, with the help of man. This revised expectation amounts to disillusionment for many. And of course no one can become too radiantly happy over a King of kings who has been stripped of His crown or a Lord of lords who has lost His sovereignty.

Another cause of the decline of expectation is hope deferred which, according to the proverb, "maketh the heart sick" (Proverbs 13:12), The modern civilized man is impatient; he takes the short-range view of things. He is surrounded by gadgets that get things done in a hurry. He was brought up on quick oats; he likes his instant coffee; he wears drip-dry shirts and takes one-minute Polaroid® snapshots of his children. His wife shops for her spring hat before the leaves are down in the fall. His new car, if he buys it after June 1, is already an old model when he brings it home. He is almost always in a hurry and can't bear to wait for anything.

This breathless way of living naturally makes for a mentality impatient of delay, and when this man enters the kingdom of God he brings his short-range psychology with him. He finds prophecy too slow for him. His first radiant expectations soon lose their luster. He is likely to inquire, "Lord, wilt Thou at this time restore again the kingdom to Israel?" and when there is no immediate response he may conclude, "My Lord delayeth His coming." The faith of Christ offers no buttons to push for quick service. The new order must wait the Lord's own time, and that is too much for the man in a hurry. He just gives up and becomes interested in something else.

Another cause is eschatological confusion. The vitalizing hope of the emergence of a new world wherein dwelleth righteousness became an early casualty in the war of conflicting prophetic interpretations. Teachers of prophecy, who knew more than the prophets they claimed to teach, debated the fine points of Scripture ad infinitum while a discouraged and disillusioned Christian public shook their heads and wondered. A leader of one evangelical group told me that his denomination had recently been, in his words, "split down the middle" over a certain small point of prophetic teaching, one incidentally which had never been heard of among the children of God until about one hundred years ago.

Certain popular views of prophecy have been discredited by events within the lifetime of some of us; a new generation of Christians cannot be blamed if their Messianic expectations are somewhat confused. When the teachers are divided, what can the pupils do?

It should be noted that there is a vast difference between the doctrine of Christ's coming and the *hope* of His coming. The first we may hold without feeling a trace of the second. Indeed there are multitudes of Christians today who hold to the doctrine of the second coming. What I have talked about here is that overwhelming sense of anticipation that lifts the life onto a new plane and fills the heart with rapturous optimism. This is what we today lack.

Frankly, I do not know whether or not it is possible to recapture the spirit of anticipation that animated the Early Church and cheered the hearts of gospel Christians only a few decades ago. Certainly scolding will not bring it back, nor arguing over prophecy, nor condemning those who do not agree with us. We may do all or any of these things without arousing the desired spirit of joyous expectation. That unifying, healing, purifying hope is for the childlike, the innocent-hearted, the unsophisticated.

Possibly nothing short of a world catastrophe that will destroy every false trust and turn our eyes once more upon the Man Christ Jesus will bring back the glorious hope to a generation that has lost it.

Choices Reveal—and Make—Character

Into nine words, having altogether but eleven syllables, Luke packs a world of universal truth: "Being let go, they went to their own company" (Acts 4:23).

Every normal man has a "company," however small, where he feels at home and to which he will return when he is tired of being alone.

The important thing about a man is not where he goes when he is compelled to go, but where he goes when he is free to go where he will.

The apostles went to jail, and that is not too revealing because they went there against their will; but when they got out of jail and could go where they would, they immediately went to the praying company. From this we learn a great deal about them. The choices of life, not the compulsions, reveal character.

A man is absent from church Sunday morning. Where is he? If he is in a hospital having his appendix removed his absence tells us nothing about him except that he is ill; but if he is out on the golf course, that tells us a lot. To go to the hospital is compulsory; to go to the golf course, voluntary. The man is free to choose and he chooses to play instead of to pray. His choice reveals what kind of man he is. Choices always do.

The difference between a slave society and a free one lies in the number of free acts possible in each as compared with acts of compulsion. No society is wholly slave, as none is wholly free, but in a free society the voluntary choices are at a maximum and the acts of compulsion relatively few. In the slave society the proportions are exactly reversed.

The true character of a people is revealed in the uses it makes of its freedoms. The slave peoples do what they are told because they are not free to do what they will. It is the free nation that reveals its character by its voluntary choices. The man who "bowed by the weight of centuries . . . leans upon his hoe and gazes on the ground" when the long day's work is over is glad to get home to supper and to bed; he has little time for anything else. But in those fortunate lands where modern machinery and labor unions have given men many free hours out of every day and at least two free days out of every week, they have time to do almost anything they will. They are free to destroy themselves by their choices, and many of them are doing just that.

There is always danger that a free nation may imperil its freedom by a series of small choices destructive of that freedom. The liberty the fathers won in blood the sons may toss away in prodigality and debilitating pleasures. Any nation which for an extended period puts pleasure before liberty is likely to lose the liberty it misused.

In the realm of religion, right choices are critically important. If we Protestant Christians would retain our freedom we dare not abuse it, and it is always to abuse freedom when we choose the easy way rather than the harder but better way. The casual indifference with which millions of Protestants view their God-blessed religious liberty is ominous. Being let go they go on weekends to the lakes and mountains and beaches to play shuffleboard, fish and sunbathe. They go where their heart is and come back to the praying company only when the bad weather drives them in. Let this continue long enough and evangelical Protestantism will be ripe for a takeover by Rome.

The Christian gospel is a message of freedom through grace and we must stand fast in the liberty wherewith Christ has made us free. But what shall we do with our freedom? The apostle Paul grieved that some of the believers of his day took advantage of their freedom and indulged the flesh in the name of Christian liberty. They threw off discipline, scorned obedience and made gods of their own bellies. It is not difficult to decide which company such as these belonged to. They revealed it by the company they kept.

Our choices reveal what kind of persons we are, but there is another side to the coin. We may, by our choices, also determine what kind of persons we will become. We humans are not only in a state of being, we are in a state of becoming; we are on a slow spiral moving gradually up or down. Here we move not singly but in companies, and we are drawn to these companies by the attraction of similarity.

I think it might be well for us to check our spiritual condition occasionally by the simple test of compatibility. When we are free to go, where do we go? In what company do we feel most at home? Where do our thoughts turn when they are free to turn where they will? When the pressure of work or business or school has temporarily lifted and we are able to think of what we will instead of what we must, what do we think of then?

The answer to these questions may tell us more about ourselves than we can comfortably accept. But we had better face up to things. We haven't too much time at the most.

The Importance
of Sound Doctrine

It would be impossible to overemphasize the importance of sound doctrine in the life of a Christian. Right thinking about all spiritual matters is imperative if we would have right living. As men do not gather grapes of thorns nor figs of thistles, so sound character does not grow out of unsound teaching.

The word *doctrine* means simply religious beliefs held and taught. It is the sacred task of all Christians, first as believers and then as teachers of religious beliefs, to be certain that these beliefs correspond exactly to truth. A precise agreement between belief and fact constitutes soundness in doctrine. We cannot afford to have less.

The apostles not only taught truth but contended for its purity against any who would cor-

rupt it. The Pauline epistles resist every effort of
false teachers to introduce doctrinal vagaries.
John's epistles are sharp with condemnation of
those teachers who harassed the young church by
denying the incarnation and throwing doubts
upon the doctrine of the Trinity; and Jude in his
brief but powerful epistle rises to heights of burning eloquence as he pours scorn upon evil teachers who would mislead the saints.

Each generation of Christians must look to its
beliefs. While truth itself is unchanging, the
minds of men are porous vessels out of which
truth can leak and into which error may seep to
dilute the truth they contain. The human heart is
heretical by nature and runs to error as naturally
as a garden to weeds. All a man, a church or a denomination needs to guarantee deterioration of
doctrine is to take everything for granted and do
nothing. The unattended garden will soon be
overrun with weeds; the heart that fails to cultivate truth and root out error will shortly be a
theological wilderness; the church or denomination that grows careless on the highway of truth
will before long find itself astray, bogged down in
some mudflat from which there is no escape.

In every field of human thought and activity
accuracy is considered a virtue. To err ever so
slightly is to invite serious loss, if not death itself.
Only in religious thought is faithfulness to truth
looked upon as a fault. When men deal with
things earthly and temporal they demand truth;
when they come to the consideration of things

heavenly and eternal they hedge and hesitate as if truth either could not be discovered or didn't matter anyway.

Montaigne said that a liar is one who is brave toward God and a coward toward men; for a liar faces God and shrinks from men. Is this not simply a proof of unbelief? Is it not to say that the liar believes in men but is not convinced of the existence of God, and is willing to risk the displeasure of a God who may not exist rather than that of man who obviously does?

I think also that deep, basic unbelief is back of human carelessness in religion. The scientist, the physician, the navigator deals with matters he knows are real; and because these things are real the world demands that both teacher and practitioner be skilled in the knowledge of them. The teacher of spiritual things only is required to be unsure in his beliefs, ambiguous in his remarks and tolerant of every religious opinion expressed by anyone, even by the man least qualified to hold an opinion.

Haziness of doctrine has always been the mark of the liberal. When the Holy Scriptures are rejected as the final authority on religious belief something must be found to take their place. Historically that something has been either reason or sentiment: if sentiment, it has been humanism. Sometimes there has been an admixture of the two, as may be seen in liberal churches today. These will not quite give up the Bible, neither will they quite believe it; the result is an unclear body of beliefs more like a fog than a mountain, where anything *may* be true but nothing may be trusted as being *certainly* true.

We have gotten accustomed to the blurred puffs of gray fog that pass for doctrine in modernistic churches and expect nothing better, but it is a cause for real alarm that the fog has begun of late to creep into many evangelical churches. From some previously unimpeachable sources are now coming vague statements consisting of a milky admixture of Scripture, science and human sentiment that is true to none of its ingredients because each one works to cancel the others out.

Certain of our evangelical brethren appear to be laboring under the impression that they are advanced thinkers because they are rethinking evolution and reevaluating various Bible doctrines or even divine inspiration itself; but so far are they from being advanced thinkers that they are merely timid followers of modernism—fifty years behind the parade.

Little by little evangelical Christians these days are being brainwashed. One evidence is that increasing numbers of them are becoming ashamed to be found unequivocally on the side of truth. They say they believe but their beliefs have been so diluted as to be impossible of clear definition.

Moral power has always accompanied definitive beliefs. Great saints have always been dogmatic. We need right now a return to a gentle dogmatism that smiles while it stands stubborn and firm on the Word of God that liveth and abideth forever.

CHAPTER

38

Some Things Are
Not Negotiable

W ill Rogers once opined that a sure way to prevent war would be to abolish peace conferences.

Of course Will, as usual, had his tongue in his cheek; he meant only to poke fun at the weak habit of substituting talk for action. Still there is more than a little uncomfortable truth in his remark.

This above all others is the age of much talk. Hardly a day passes that the newspapers do not carry one or another of the headlines "Talks to Begin" or "Talks to Continue" or "Talks to Resume." The notion back of this endless official chatter is that all differences between men result from their failure to understand each other; if each can discover exactly what the other thinks they will find to their delight that they are really in full agreement after all. Then they have only to smile, shake hands, go home and live happily ever after.

At the bottom of all this is the glutinous, one-world, all-men-are-brothers philosophy that has taken such hold on the minds of many of our educators and politicians. (The hardheaded realists of the communist camp know better; maybe that is why they are making such alarming advances throughout the world while the all-men-are-brothers devotees are marring around in confusion, trying to keep smiling if it kills them.)

Tolerance, charity, understanding, good will, patience and other such words and ideas are lifted from the Bible, misunderstood and applied indiscriminately to every situation. The kidnapper will not steal your baby if you only try to understand him; the burglar caught sneaking into your house with a gun is not really bad; he is just hungry for fellowship and togetherness; the gang killer taking his victim for a one-way ride can be dissuaded from committing murder if someone will only have faith in his basic goodness and have a talk with him. And this is supposed to be the teaching of Jesus, which it most certainly is not.

The big thing now is to "keep in touch." Never let the dialogue die and never accept any decision as final; everything can be negotiated. Where there is life there is talk and where there is talk there is hope. "As long as they are talking they are not shooting at each other," say the advocates of the long palaver, and in so saying they forget Pearl Harbor.

This yen to confer has hit the Church also, which is not strange since almost everything the Church is doing these days has been suggested to her by the world. I observe with pained amusement how many water boys of the pulpit in their effort to be prophets are standing up straight and tall and speaking out boldly in favor of ideas that have been previously fed into their minds by the psychiatrists, the sociologists, the novelists, the scientists and the secular educators. The ability to appraise correctly the direction public opinion is moving is a gift not to be despised; by means of it we preachers can talk loudly and still stay out of trouble.

A new Decalogue has been adopted by the neo-Christians of our day, the first word of which reads, "Thou shalt not disagree"; and a new set of Beatitudes too, which begins, "Blessed are they that tolerate everything, for they shall not be made accountable for anything." It is now the accepted thing to talk over religious differences in public with the understanding that no one will try to convert another or point out errors in his belief. The purpose of these talks is not to confront truth, but to discover how the followers of other religions think and thus benefit from their views as we hope they will from ours.

It is a truism that people agree to disagree only about matters they consider unimportant. No man is tolerant when it concerns his life or the life of his child, and no one will agree to negotiate over any religious matter he considers vital to his eternal welfare. Imagine Moses agreeing to take part in a panel discussion with Israel over the golden calf; or Elijah engaging in a gentlemanly dialogue with the prophets of Baal. Or try to picture our Lord Jesus Christ seeking a meeting of minds with the Pharisees to iron out differences; or Athanasius trying to rise above his differences with Arius in order to achieve union on a higher level; or Luther crawling into the presence of the pope in the name of a broader Christian fellowship.

The desire to be liked even if not respected is a great weakness in any man's character, and in that of a minister of Jesus Christ it is a weakness wholly inexcusable. The popular image of the man of God as a smiling, congenial, asexual religious mascot whose handshake is always soft and whose head is always bobbing in the perpetual Yes of universal acquiescence is not the image found in the Scriptures of truth.

The blessing of God is promised to the peacemaker, but the religious negotiator had better watch his step. The ability to settle quarrels between members of God's household is a heavenly gift and one that should be assiduously cultivated. The discerning soul who can reconcile separated friends by prayer and appeal to the Scriptures is worth his weight in diamonds.

That is one thing, but the effort to achieve unity at the expense of truth and righteousness is another. To seek to be friends with those who will not be the friends of Christ is to be a traitor to our Lord. Darkness and light can never be brought together by talk. Some things are not negotiable.

CHAPTER

39

The Saint Must Walk Alone

M ost of the world's great souls have been lonely. Loneliness seems to be one price the saint must pay for his saintliness.

In the morning of the world (or should we say, in that strange darkness that came soon after the dawn of man's creation) that pious soul, Enoch, walked with God and was not, for God took him; and while it is not stated in so many words, a fair inference is that Enoch walked a path quite apart from his contemporaries.

Another lonely man was Noah who, of all the antediluvians, found grace in the sight of God; and every shred of evidence points to the aloneness of his life even while surrounded by his people.

Again, Abraham had Sarah and Lot, as well as many servants and herdmen, but who can read his story and the apostolic comment upon it without sensing instantly that he was a man "whose soul was alike a star and dwelt apart"? As far as we know, not one word did God ever speak to him in the company of men. Facedown he communed with his God, and the innate dignity of the man forbade that he assume this posture in the presence of others. How sweet and solemn was the scene that night of the sacrifice when he saw the lamps of fire moving between the pieces of offering. There alone with a horror of great darkness upon him he heard the voice of God and knew that he was a man marked for divine favor.

Moses also was a man apart. While yet attached to the court of Pharaoh he took long walks alone, and during one of these walks while far removed from the crowds he saw an Egyptian and a Hebrew fighting and came to the rescue of his countryman. After the resultant break with Egypt he dwelt in almost complete seclusion in the desert. There while he watched his sheep alone the wonder of the burning bush appeared to him, and later on the peak of Sinai he crouched alone to gaze in fascinated awe at the Presence, partly hidden, partly disclosed, within the cloud and fire.

The prophets of pre-Christian times differed widely from each other, but one mark they bore in common was their enforced loneliness. They loved their people and gloried in the religion of the fathers, but their loyalty to the God of Abraham, Isaac and Jacob and their zeal for the welfare of the nation of Israel drove them away from the crowd and into long periods of heaviness. "I am become a stranger unto my brethren, and an alien unto my mother's children" (Psalm 69:8), cried one, and unwittingly spoke for all the rest.

Most revealing of all is the sight of that One of whom Moses and all the prophets did write, treading His lonely way to the cross, His deep loneliness unrelieved by the presence of the multitudes.

> *Tis midnight, and on Olive's brow*
> *The star is dimmed that lately shone;*
> *'Tis midnight in the garden now,*
> *The suffering Saviour prays alone.*

> *'Tis midnight, and from all removed,*
> *The Saviour wrestles lone with fears—*
> *E'en the disciple whom He loved*
> *Heeds not his Master's grief and tears.*
> —William B. Tappan

He died alone in the darkness, hidden from the sight of mortal man, and no one saw Him when He arose triumphant and walked out of the tomb, though many saw Him afterward and bore witness to what they saw.

There are some things too sacred for any eye but God's to look upon. The curiosity, the clamor, the well-meant but blundering effort to help can only hinder the waiting soul and make unlikely, if not impossible, the communication of the secret message of God to the worshiping heart.

Sometimes we react by a kind of religious reflex and repeat dutifully the proper words and phrases even though they fail to express our real feelings and lack the authenticity of personal experience.

Right now is such a time. A certain conventional loyalty may lead some who hear this unfamiliar truth expressed for the first time to say brightly, "Oh, I am never lonely. Christ said, 'I will never leave thee, nor forsake thee,' (Hebrews 13:5) and, 'Lo, I am with you alway' (Matthew 28:20). How can I be lonely when Jesus is with me?"

Now I do not want to reflect on the sincerity of any Christian soul, but this stock testimony is too neat to be real. It is obviously what the speaker thinks should be true rather than what he has proved to be true by the test of experience. This cheerful denial of loneliness proves only that the speaker has never walked with God without the support and encouragement afforded him by society. The sense of companionship which he mistakenly attributes to the presence of Christ may and probably does arise from the presence of friendly people. Always remember: You cannot carry a cross in company. Though a man were surrounded by a vast crowd, his cross is his alone and his carrying of it marks him as a man apart. Society has turned against him; otherwise he would have no cross. No one is a friend to the man with a cross. "They all forsook him, and fled" (Mark 14:50).

The pain of loneliness arises from the constitution of our nature. God made us for each other. The desire for human companionship is completely natural and right. The loneliness of the Christian results from his walk with God in an ungodly world, a walk that must often take him away from the fellowship of good Christians as well as from that of the unregenerate world. His God-given instincts cry out for companionship with others of his kind, others who can understand his longings, his aspirations, his absorption in the love of Christ; and because within his circle of friends there are so few who share his inner experiences he is forced to walk alone. The unsatisfied longings of the prophets for human understanding caused them to cry out in their complaint, and even our Lord Himself suffered in the same way.

The man who has passed on into the divine Presence in actual inner experience will not find many who understand him. A certain amount of social fellowship will of course be his as he mingles with religious persons in the regular activities of the church, but true spiritual fellowship will be hard to find. But he should not expect things to be otherwise. After all, he is a stranger and a pilgrim, and the journey he takes is not on his feet but in his heart. He walks with God in the garden of his own soul—and who but God can walk there with him? He is of another spirit from the multitudes that tread the courts of the Lord's house. He has seen that of which they have only heard, and he walks among them somewhat as Zacharias walked after his return from the altar when the people whispered, "He has seen a vision" (see Luke 1:22).

The truly spiritual man is indeed something of an oddity. He lives not for himself but to promote the interests of Another. He seeks to persuade people to give all to his Lord and asks no portion or share for himself. He delights not to be honored but to see his

Savior glorified in the eyes of men. His joy is to see his Lord promoted and himself neglected. He finds few who care to talk about that which is the supreme object of his interest, so he is often silent and preoccupied in the midst of noisy religious shoptalk. For this he earns the reputation of being dull and overserious, so he is avoided and the gulf between him and society widens. He searches for friends upon whose garments he can detect the smell of myrrh and aloes and cassia out of the ivory palaces, and finding few or none he, like Mary of old, keeps these things in his heart.

It is this very loneliness that throws him back upon God. "When my father and my mother forsake me, then the LORD will take me up" (Psalm 27:10). His inability to find human companionship drives him to seek in God what he can find nowhere else. He learns in inner solitude what he could not have learned in the crowd—that Christ is All in all, that He is made unto us wisdom, righteousness, sanctification and redemption, that in Him we have and possess life's *summum bonum*.

Two things remain to be said. One, that the lonely man of whom we speak is not a haughty man, nor is he the holier-than-thou, austere saint so bitterly satirized in popular literature. He is likely to feel that he is the least of all men and is sure to blame himself for his very loneliness. He wants to share his feelings with others and to open his heart to some like-minded soul—who will understand him, but the spiritual climate around him does not encourage it, so he remains silent and tells his griefs to God alone.

The second thing is that the lonely saint is not the withdrawn man who hardens himself against human suffering and spends his days contemplating the heavens. Just the opposite is true. His loneliness makes him sympathetic to the approach of the brokenhearted and the fallen and the sin-bruised. Because he is detached from the world he is all the more able to help it. Meister Eckhart taught his followers that if they should find themselves in prayer, as it were, caught up to the third heavens, and happen to remember that a poor widow needed food, they should break off the prayer instantly and go care for the widow. "God will not suffer you to lose anything by it," he told them. "You can take up again in prayer where you left off and the Lord will make it up to you." This is typical of the great mystics and masters of the interior life from Paul to the present day.

The weakness of so many modern Christians is that they feel too much at home in the world. In their effort to achieve restful "adjustment" to unregenerate society they have lost their pilgrim character and become an essential part of the very moral order against which they are sent to protest. The world recognizes them and accepts them for what they are. And this is the saddest thing that can be said about them. They are not lonely, but neither are they saints.

This chapter was written for Eternity Magazine *and is used here with their kind permission.*

TITLES BY A.W. TOZER